LET GOD ARISE

LET GOD ARISE

by

RICHARD HOLLOWAY

'Let God arise, and let his enemies be scattered.'

Psalm 68

LONDON: A. R. MOWBRAY & CO LTD
NEW YORK: MOREHOUSE–BARLOW CO

Text set in 14pt Monotype Bembo, printed by letterpress,
and bound in Great Britain at The Pitman Press, Bath

ISBN 0 264 64598 7

First published 1972
by A. R. Mowbray & Co Ltd
The Alden Press, Osney Mead,
Oxford, OX2 OEG

TO JEANNIE

CONTENTS

vii

ACKNOWLEDGEMENTS

The thanks of the author and publishers are due to the following for permission to quote extracts: Methuen & Co Ltd, *Concerning the Inner Life* by Evelyn Underhill; The Seabury Press Inc, *The Magnificent Defeat* by Frederick Buechner; Herder & Herder, *The Church as Mission* by Eugene Hillman.

All Biblical quotations from the Jerusalem Bible, by permission of Darton, Longman and Todd; from The New English Bible, second edition, © 1970, by permission of the Oxford and Cambridge University Presses. I would like to acknowledge my debt to Professor John Macquarrie, now Lady Margaret Professor in the University of Oxford, not only for permission to quote extracts from his writings, but for his friendship and influence over several years, especially while I studied at Union Theological Seminary in New York.

I also owe a debt of gratitude to Canon William Purcell who encouraged me to finish this book at a time when pressure of work tempted me to give it up. In the same connection, I must thank my wife and the other residents of Lauder House whose good-humoured support helped me to make time for writing.

Finally, I would like to thank Miss Carol Gigg for transforming my grubby typescript into copy ready for the printer.

R.H.

So, when the crowd gives tongue
And prophets, old or young,
Bawl out their strange despair
Or fall in worship there,
Let them applaud the image or condemn
But keep your distance and your soul from them.
And, if the heart within your breast must burst
Like a cracked crucible and pour its steel
White-hot before the white heat of the wheel,
Strive to recast once more
That attar of the ore
In the strong mould of pain
Till it is whole again,
And while the prophets shudder or adore
Before the flame, hoping it will give ear,
If you at last must have a word to say,
Say neither, in their way
'It is a deadly magic and accursed,'
Nor 'It is blest,' but only 'It is here.'

John Brown's Body
Stephen Vincent Benet

PART ONE

1

Ghetto or Surrender?

THE TEMPTATION to do itself to death has always been an occupational hazard for the Church. Psychologists have suggested that suicide may be a life-affirming act, an act of creative despair, a violent grasp at immortality. Whether true or not, such theories suggest a way to understand the Church's permanent impulse to self-destruction. Within every attempt at ecclesiastical suicide is hidden an affirmation of indestructible life. The Church is endlessly engaged in giving up its life in order to save it. The process is irritating, but it seems to be a necessity.

The destructive impulses in the Church's history have usually been caused by an attempt to resolve an unresolvable tension: the tension between worship and mission, the enjoyment of God and the service of man; the tension, so old in religion, between priest and prophet. The Church exists in history to bear witness to the glorious reality of God. It stands in time as a priestly community, set part as a sign of an overwhelming yet invisible reality, yet it is sent to make disciples of all nations: it is sent into the world with a message for all the world. Pursuing the roles of

3

mission and worship places the Church in a state of permanent and creative tension. The Church is placed, for all time, in a permanent tension between *ghetto* and *surrender*. I use the words in a neutral way, though for most people they will unavoidably be laden with unattractive associations. The *ghetto* fulfilled a necessary and important function in history. It was a place where the Jew could practise his religion and preserve his culture. The continued existence of the Jewish people down the ages, despite centuries of persecution, is testimony to the effectiveness of the ghetto. *Surrender* too, can be a necessary response; it can be the resolution of a wearying and pointless stand-off; it can set the context for a more important kind of triumph. The Christian Church stands in a necessary tension between the two poles. Almost all theology and a great deal of Church history can be explained by such tension.

In the first century the Church was what sociologists call a cognitive minority, that is, a group of people whose view of the world differs significantly from the one generally taken for granted in their society.[1] Cognitive minorities may react in either of two ways to the pressures of the alien society in which they are set. (1) They may retreat from contact with society into a ghetto where they meet only their own kind, where their minority status is disguised, and where they can find social support for their characteristic beliefs. Any group which believes itself to possess some distinguishing truth is obviously interested in the preservation of that truth. The ghetto is a very effective method of preservation. Modern examples are provided by the Close Brethren, an exclusivist sect which is found in some fishing villages in the North East of Scotland, and the Amish, who retain a horse and buggy culture in the midst of modern America. (2) The other response is surrender to the alien culture. This surrender may take place unconsciously at first. The threatened minority can retain its own vocabulary long after it has surrendered the beliefs the vocabulary once conveyed. That is why Alasdair Macintyre said John Robinson combined a religious vocabulary with substantive atheism.

The fascinating thing about the Church is that, appearances to the contrary, it has never entirely given in to either alternative. It has not, I believe, because the Church has always held itself to be a missionary body. It has always claimed to possess information, news of urgent and intense concern to all men everywhere. Christian tradition is full of images of men running to bring beleaguered villagers news of victory, of feet pounding over mountains, impatient with glad tidings. The command, 'make disciples of all nations,' contained several fateful implications. On the one hand, the Christian evangelist was heir to a message, a particular piece of news. Corresponding to the given element was the need to preserve the message by containing it safely within a supporting structure where the believer could be preserved from the temptation to surrender it to the pressure of the larger culture. On the other hand was the command to spread the message, to make it known among the nations, which made necessary a constant interaction between the Church and society, and which put the Church permanently at risk. There would be a constant temptation to dissolve the Church's message into the dominant worldview, what is usually called, 'the spirit of the age'. Modern sociologists describe such surrender as going native: the adherent of the minority position gradually succumbs to the assault of the majority view and ends by embracing, if at first unconsciously, the view he set out to challenge. So the Christian Church found itself in a permanent tension between ghetto and surrender, between isolation and going native. In this part of the book I shall have more to say about the phenomenon of ecclesiastical surrender because it is the theme of a very vocal and influential group of theologians today. In a later section I shall examine the need to restate the ghetto theme in the Church's life.

An early example of the creative use of tension in the Church's life is found in the missionary work of the apostle Paul. Paul faced the fundamental difficulty of every evangelist, the problem of communication.

The very fact that he could talk to men about God at all indicated that he recognised no fundamental discontinuity between the experience of men and the reality of God. *Theo-logy*, that is, 'God-talk,' was possible. The words of men could communicate to other men something of the reality of God because man was made with an innate sense of the reality of God, however cloudy or confused it might be. The problem was to find the right words or the correct analogies within the experience of the hearers to break open for them the Reality imprisoned within them. It is important to stress the relationship of continuity between man and God because without it evangelism is useless. If God is 'wholly Other', as some theologians say, if he is a language no man understands, then the whole missionary enterprise is false because it is based on the possibility of talking about God to men and being understood. Whether indeed most men understand God-talk today we must discuss later, but there can be no doubt that Paul assumed that they did in his time. God's truth, Paul believed, was active in germ in man's life, so no evangelist came into a situation that was completely unprepared for him. Luke reports a good example.

The one amusement the Athenians and the foreigners living there seem to have, apart from discussing the latest ideas, is listening to lectures about them. So Paul stood before the whole Council of the Areopagus and made this speech: 'Men of Athens, I have seen for myself how extremely scrupulous you are in all religious matters, because I noticed, as I strolled round admiring your sacred monuments, that you had an altar inscribed: "To an Unknown God." Well, the God whom I proclaim is in fact the one whom you already worship without knowing it.' (Acts 17.21–23)

Paul was a convinced exponent of what is now called *natural theology*. God was no stranger to men. His reality was a constant pressure on their lives, even though they perceived it in scattered and fragmented ways. In the fifth century St Augustine described his experience in the burning words of his *Confessions*:

> They fled that they might not see thee, who sawest them; that they might be blinded and stumble into thee . . . For in truth they do not know that thou art everywhere; that no place contains thee, and that only thou art near even to those who go farthest from thee. Let them turn back and seek thee—and lo, thou art there in their hearts, there in the hearts of those who confess to thee. Let them cast themselves upon thee . . . after all their weary wanderings. . . . And where was I when I was seeking thee? There thou wast, before me; but I had gone away, even from myself, and I could not find myself, much less thee.[2]

The peculiar anguish of the evangelist at all times and in all places is to find the word that will reveal to men the reality whom they have been unconsciously seeking and ignorantly worshipping. The evangelist is placed under a permanent discipline of identification with those to whom he is sent. He has to go native, become all things to all men, without surrendering the integrity of his message.

> Though I am not a slave of any man I have made myself the slave of everyone so as to win as many as I could. I made myself a Jew to the Jews, to win the Jews. . . For the weak I made myself weak. I made myself all things to all men in order to save some at any cost; and I still do this, for the sake of the gospel and to have a share in its blessings. (1 Corinthians 9.19 ff.)

The discipline of identification has been the mark of the great missionary since Paul's day. Gregory the Great advised his missionaries to Britain to sanctify rather than to destroy the existing cultures in which they would minister. Heathen temples were to be detached from the service of the Devil and adapted to the service of God. Pagan feasts were to be turned into Christian feasts. But we have to recognise again and again the great risks to the message in that evangelistic imperative. There was the constant temptation to merge the message into the prevailing worldview for the sake of a smooth transition from false belief to faith. No smooth transition is possible. There is a critical point at which a decision has to be made. I have stressed the continuity between God and man, because only so is evangelism possible; but there is an essential distance, a discontinuity, a gap, that no bridge can span. The evangelist can bring a man to the gap. He cannot carry him over.

Throughout history there have been men, and

usually men with a burning zeal for their fellows, who have tried to remove the gap. One of the motives behind the repeated attempts to smooth transition from false belief to faith has been a mistaken conviction that the Christian faith was destined to include the whole of mankind. That is an understandable fantasy for the zealous evangelist, but it is a fantasy nevertheless. What of Matthew 26.19: 'Go, therefore, make disciples of all the nations, baptise them in the name of the Father and of the Son and of the Holy Spirit, and teach them to observe all the commands I gave you. And know that I am with you always; yes, to the end of time'? Surely it is not the nations who are to become disciples, but people within the nations. The Church is a representative community, drawn out from all the nations of the earth, signifying an invisible reality. It is not a triumphalist organisation, intent on absorbing the world, but a serving, representative community, set up in history as a sign of the final rule of God. It is a sign that is stained and tattered, a sign that is frequently spoken against, but a sign nevertheless of the glory of God and the destiny of man. It follows therefore, that the Church will stand in history as a representative minority, a priesthood of believers whose lives are offered on behalf of those who do not yet believe. Yet that priestly, representative community is placed under the inescapable command to make disciples from among the nations. The tensions of its double vocation are obvious and there have always been Christians whose zeal has led them to try to resolve the tension on one side or the other, ghetto or surrender. For centuries the Church has characteristically engaged in building itself into a ghetto. In our day we are witnessing the bursting of the ghetto. The characteristic activity of Christian theologians today is, not ghetto, but surrender.

2

The Surrender of Theology

SINCE PAUL's day Christian theologians have followed him in attempting to interpret the Christian faith
to its 'cultured despisers' (the term invented by
Schleiermacher in 1799). Unfortunately, they have
often ceased to follow Paul and begun to follow the
critics they were trying to win.

> Increasingly, Protestant theology has oriented itself by
> changing coteries of 'cultured despisers' of religion, that
> is, by shifting groups of secularised intellectuals whose
> respect it solicited and whose cognitive presuppositions
> it accepted as binding. In other words, Protestant theolo-
> gians have been increasingly engaged in playing a game
> whose rules have been dictated by their cognitive
> antagonists. While this curious vulnerability (not to say
> lack of character) can probably be explained sociologi-
> cally, what is interesting here is the over-all result—a
> profound erosion of the traditional religious contents, in
> extreme cases to the point where nothing is left but
> hollow rhetoric. Of late it seems more and more as if the
> extreme has become the norm.[1]

Theology, like the Church, is in a perpetual tension
between surrendering its own integrity and going
native by accepting the prevailing worldview, or of
fossilising by retreating into an intellectual ghetto

where it can preserve itself from the acids of unbelief.

Christian faith has, from the beginning, taken for granted the reality of what is usually called 'the supernatural.'

> . . . the term, particularly in its everyday usage, denotes a fundamental category of religion, namely the assertion or belief that there is *an other reality*, and one of ultimate significance for man, which transcends the reality within which our everyday experience unfolds.[2]

The Church claims to possess a message which relates to a specific set of interactions between the supernatural reality and the reality experienced in our everyday lives. The interactions concern the events in the life of Jesus Christ. The 'cultured despiser' of religion today totally rejects the supernatural, presenting the accommodating theologian with a major evangelical embarrassment. If the fundamental premise of your message is rejected, where can dialogue begin? Certain theologians begin the dialogue by themselves rejecting the premise. They are then able to address themselves to the world in the world's own language. What have they left to say? A very great deal, as it turns out.

One of the earliest examples of such going native can be found in the writings of R. M. Braithwaite. Braithwaite neatly stands traditional Christian belief on its head. The Church has always been concerned about conduct, about ethics. In traditional Christian thinking, however, ethics have always been derivative: they follow from our relationship with God. Indeed, Paul maintained that the power as well as the intention to act rightly came from God alone. Our good acts are the result of our faith. This was the message delivered by Paul, but it is profoundly embarrassing to a culture that repudiates the reality of God and the supernatural. Braithwaite resolves the embarrassment by surrendering the argument.

> To say that it is belief in the dogmas of religion which is the cause of the believer's intending to behave as he does is to put the cart before the horse: it is the intention to behave which constitutes what is known as religious conviction.[3]

Braithwaite knows that the Christian message is more than a series of moral imperatives. There are many embarrassing 'dogmas of religion', as he calls them, on which the imperatives are supposedly based. He disposes of the dogmas by denying that they give any information about reality at all. Instead, he maintains, they provide a useful psychological crutch to support our intention to behave: 'A religious belief is an intention to behave in a certain way (a moral belief) together with the entertainment of certain stories associated with the intention in the mind of the believer.'[4]

In other words, when I say 'God is love', I don't really mean that *God* is love. I'm not really saying any thing about God at all. I mean that *I* want to be loving and believe that the repetition of the three words will help me to fulfil that intention. Such religious statements are reduced to semantic mascots carried round by certain people who call themselves Christians, much as racing drivers carry rabbit tails.

Braithwaite's scheme is an entertaining example of how vacuous theology can become when translated without remainder into what Berger calls 'the cognitive presuppositions' of its cultured despisers. We are left with certain earnest individuals who egg themselves on to good behaviour by systematically entertaining in their minds a series of statements which they know to be substantially meaningless. The Christian message is reduced to an eccentric word-game. Any self-respecting despiser of religion is bound to reply to an invitation to join in such a venture, 'Why bother?' Why indeed?

A much more interesting example of the theology of surrender is contained in Harvey Cox's book, *The Secular City*. Cox's programme is far more complicated than Braithwaite's and far less open to the charge of complete surrender to the cognitive fashion of the moment. Nevertheless, his is a breathtakingly novel example of an evangelism translated into the dominant cultural motif of its day. The fact that today, six years after the event, it is curiously dated and beside the point makes an examination of it all the more relevant.

The really new thing in Cox's book is the enthusiastic identification of the modern, secular city with the Kingdom of God. Of course, he would hasten to add, the kingdom is not yet completely realised in history, but the city is the most complete manifestation of the Kingdom of God that history has yet afforded. History is seen as the gradual unfolding of some ultimate, urban revelation. The key ingredient in the unfolding process has been the ethical element in biblical religion. Ethics is always a safe card to play in the game of dialogue with the liberal-minded cultured despiser of religion. According to Cox, the ethical element in religion was the acid which dissolved, in time, man's immature dependence on the supernatural. The world has been disenchanted and man can now enjoy it without reference to any transcendent reality which shapes his ends. There is no ghost left in the machine. Man is in charge at last.

I have great difficulty when someone confidently sets out exactly what history is up to. To detect a grand design in history, especially one so flattering to modern man, you have to ignore an enormous amount of material. Richard Rubinstein points out that to accept the notion that everything that happens in history is part of the process of the kingdom realising itself 'would involve seeing evidence of the Kingdom in such expressions of contemporary technopolis as Auschwitz, which was a highly rational, technopolitan factory for the manufacture of corpses.'[5]

It would be just as possible to write a book demonstrating how the modern secular city, with its alienation, impersonalism, and violence is the ultimate outreach of the demonic man, the last stage before man's dissolution. What Cox offers is not a theology of the city, but the secular city as theology. The roots of his thinking are found, not in the Bible but in the cultural milieu that he inhabited while writing *The Secular City*—the intoxicating atmosphere of white liberal America during the days of John Kennedy's presidency. He wrote at a particularly winsome time, when it was widely believed that men of goodwill could weld the kingdom out of the raw materials of history. The civil rights movement, of which Cox was a particularly courageous participant, seemed about to alter the face of America for the better. 'We Shall Overcome' sounds strangely tame and wistful today: in the early sixties it was sung with an evangelical optimism. American self-confidence was in full and good-humoured flood. Things are very different today. John and Robert Kennedy have been killed. Martin Luther King has been killed. American cities have suffered riot and revolution. Confidence in American righteousness and power have led step by step into Vietnam. The confident optimism of *The Secular City* seems beside the point—or worse, a cause of present tragedies.

Another major cultural influence on Cox is the overturning of a long-standing anti-urban bias in

American history and culture. Until this century most Americans lived in the country, in farm, village or small town. The city was evil. It was the source of corruption. Largely in our own era the middle-class American has discovered that the invigorating complexities of urban living can be enjoyed and not just endured. In many cases it amounts to a sort of urban conversion experience. For a while in the best American theological seminaries there was a new puritanism. Everyone wanted to work in 'the inner city'. The young seminarian accepted a post in suburb or small town only with guilt, and spent his ministry there flogging his congregation as suburban captives or prisoners of the past. It was heady stuff. I suspect that Cox embraced the city with the ardour of a Primitive Baptist discovering the pleasures of the bottle after a lifetime of abstinence.

Clive Entwistle, an architect and city planner, began a review of a massive work called *Taming Megalapolis* with these words:

> There is a Sufi teaching story about a mouse that climbed onto the head of an elephant and imagined itself to be its mahout. To preserve the illusion of control the mouse-mahout programmed his commands to follow the movements of the great beast which was, of course, unaware of his presence. It is in this nursery sense only that the title 'Taming Megalapolis' can be applied to these two volumes of papers.[6]

So much for the Coxian notion that man is in charge of the secular city. Entwistle goes on to point out that the term *megalapolis* was coined by Jean Gottman in 1961 to describe the vast urban and suburban conglomeration that sprawls over some five hundred miles of the northeastern seaboard of the USA. It is, he says, 'the present habitat of some forty million Americans. It is still expanding, at an increasing rate, without benefit of conscious control, direction or evaluation.'[7]

The secular city has become, in fact, the American nightmare. Already cities are disfigured with the hideous symptoms of cultural degeneration. Outside of London, perhaps, British cities haven't yet reached that stage of terminal chaos which is the mark of the secular city in America. We still have a little time in which to control and humanise British cities, but Cox's urban mysticism won't help us much. Dean Inge once remarked that a man who marries the spirit of the age soon finds himself a widower. Cox's book is a particularly instructive example of what happens to a theology that marries the spirit of the age.

As we would expect, Cox was soon considered passé by the theologically fashionable, who moved on to the theme of 'Revolution,' dismissing Cox as a mere 'reformist theologian.' Even so, revolutionary theology is the same old thing. The theologian has merely traded his mod suit for a Mao shirt and Che Guevara hairstyle. We are not offered a theology of revolution, but revolution as theology, as Braithwaite offered ethics as theology and Cox offered the secular city.

> A theology of revolution begins with an evaluation of revolution but it must go on to a dialectical relationship between theology and revolution. *This results not in a theological evaluation of revolution, but in a revolutionising of theology.*[8]

That, at least is candid, but it makes the theologian a quick-change artist, endlessly struggling into the fashion of the moment. There is something deeply sad about a discipline so characterless, so fundamentally insecure, that it continually echoes the latest sound from the liberal intellectual establishment. C. S. Lewis once said that he'd never heard of anyone being converted from unbelief to any of the currently fashionable versions of secular theology. Why would anyone want to play code-games with theologians who echo his own worldview? Anyone who retains a nostalgic fondness for the traditional Christian vocabulary is unlikely to respond to the mod versions. To the cultured despiser, the combination of substantial atheism with a religious vocabulary has no appeal at all. In a few years time the vocabulary won't be around either. Like the grin from the Cheshire cat, the vocabulary, separated from its base, will fade. The surrender will be complete.

3

The Surrender of The Church

THE SECULARISATION of theology in the sense discussed in the first two chapters has had a profound effect on the life of the Church. The erosion of the Church's understanding of itself as a sign pointing to a supernatural reality which embraces man, whether or not he recognises it, has resulted in a failure of nerve on the part of institutional Christianity. Nevertheless, like all human institutions, the Church is reluctant to face its own dissolution, even though its leaders have come to doubt the ends which it existed to serve. It has lost the vivid awareness of its supernatural meaning but is not prepared to wind up its affairs. Instead, the official Church today seems intent on discovering *social* validation for its existence. There can be little doubt that the Church today has more genuine concern for the needs of the world than at any other time in its history—a fact that is in a way, rather hopeful and important. Today, the Church understands itself as a Samaritan Church, called to the service of the suffering. But I suspect that the Samaritan task is something of an escape, because good works provide an immediate validation for the Church's existence: ethics, unlike the supernatural, is still a respectable token of exchange among the cultured despisers of religion. The more uneasy you become with the Church's traditional taint of supernaturalism, the more passionate you become in validating its empirical status through service. You fastidiously avoid any mention of the Church's supernatural credentials, indeed you cross sea and land to avoid making a single convert. Instead, you call Christians to the new ascetism of political and social commitment. To say that the Church's present preoccupation with social and political goals indicates a failure of nerve is a very grave charge and I do not make it lightly. At its highest, the present trend is good as far as it goes—but it is only a selective obedience to the Church's Founder.

If we can develop the claim made in the first chapter, that the Church is in a permanent tension between worship and mission, the priestly and the prophetical, we shall perhaps understand how surrender in the life of the Church takes place. We said that theology had two poles. On the one hand is the celebration and contemplation of the faith once delivered to the saints. Theology has a genuinely custodial role. According to Paul, the Christian gospel is not a human 'philosophy, the outreach of man's intellect: it is a revelation. There is a devastatingly unilateral quality about the gospel:

> For Christ did not send me to baptise, but to preach the Good News, and not preach that in the terms of

philosophy in which the crucifixion of Christ cannot be expressed. The language of the cross may be illogical to those who are not on the way to salvation, but those of us who are on the way see it as God's power to save. As scripture says: I shall destroy the wisdom of the wise and bring to nothing all the learning of the learned. Where are the philosophers now? Where are the scribes? Where are any of our thinkers today? Do you see now how God has shown up the foolishness of human wisdom? If it was God's wisdom that human wisdom should not know God, it was because God wanted to save those who have faith through the foolishness of the message that we preach. And so, while the Jews demand miracles and the Greeks look for wisdom, here are we preaching a crucified Christ; to the Jews an obstacle that they cannot get over, to the pagans madness, but to those who have been called, whether they are Jews or Greeks, a Christ who is the power and the wisdom of God. For God's Foolishness is wiser than human wisdom, and God's weakness is stronger than human strength. (1 Corinthians 1.17 ff.)

It is this utterly given quality in the Christian message that makes it a perennial scandal to every liberal intellectual establishment. The Gospel is not a human utterance; it is a divine utterance. The Church makes the exhorbitant claim to possess and to be possessed by a Divine Word. Popularity or unpopularity does not affect the claim. The Church may be destined to be swamped by the tides of history. No matter. The Word stands. It may be that in a hundred years time that Word will be in the custody of two old ladies sitting among their memories. No matter. The Church is raised in history as a sign of a reality independent of man's apprehension of it. That sign will stand till the end of time in market place or catacomb.

The Church has, of course, more than a custodial role. It is commanded also to spread the knowledge of its message. The Word committed to the Church is not *wholly* Other. Man is made to be able to apprehend the reality to which the Church points. This theme will be developed at greater length in another chapter, but we must note for now that the Church is under obedience to interact with man and society. The cross aptly symbolises the gospel: it comes down vertically from God and it reaches out horizontally to man. Corresponding to the Church's horizontal role is the command not only to translate the message into man's language, but to engage with man in his world. This tension gives rise to a whole cluster of antitheses in the Church's life: adoration and service; prayer and good works; God and the neighbour.

The Church today seems profoundly embarrassed with the vertical element in its task. We have suggested how in theology that various attempts to translate the message have only turned it into the conventional wisdom of the day, have turned the Divine Word into a human word. The motive has been a genuine concern to be obedient to the missionary imperative, but the result has been a gospel that has become a vacuous echo of what the world already thinks.

A subtle example of this process is provided by an

increasingly influential movement in the Church to-day. Embarrassed by the uncomfortably *given* element in the Gospel, that movement substitutes the theory of the open Canon. The Canon is the technical term that describes the New Testament scriptures that contain, for traditional Christianity, the definitive revelation of God. The Canon is now closed. The Revelation is complete. Not that the Church has ever believed that man's apprehension of the Revelation is closed—our Lord assured the Church that the Holy Spirit would be present always to guide it into ever newer apprehensions of that truth which was once delivered to it. Nevertheless, there is an ineradicably final quality about the Gospel. A new thing has happened and the Church stands in history as a witness to it. It has to be stated with considerable firmness, that the Church purports to be about something that has effectively happened; it points to an event of cosmic and eternal significance. God has acted. The Word has uttered. And nothing can ever be the same again.

Obviously, these strange and mystical claims are hilariously irrelevant to the cultured despiser of religion. If you accept the cognitive presuppositions of such a man then you must discover a *new* Canon, a more acceptable revelation, a more relevant set of finalities. So the Canon is declared open and one sets about discerning the current revelations of God. It will come as no surprise that God's action is detectable with almost uncanny precision in those areas that currently excite the interest of the average left-wing University don. A number of years ago Peter Simple, the London newspaper columnist, dismissed the kind of political liberal who turned up at protest demonstrations as a member of 'Rentacrowd'. As a long-standing member of that particular fraternity I know exactly what he means. There are a number of 'areas of concern' that activate certain people: peace, hunger, housing, capital punishment, homosexual law reform, the population explosion, racialism. Go to a meeting on any of these subjects and you meet the same old faces—and not unworthily. God is interested in all those things. The novel thing about 'rentacrowd' theology, however, is its assumption, almost without discussion, that these concerns constitute a new Canon, a new focus of revelation and, moreover, that God is undialectically forcing the world towards a left-wing solution of such perennial problems. The Church, we are told with great seriousness, is 'God's avant garde.'

It is no accident that such theology proceeds from a passionate concern for the mission of the Church. Ian Fraser, in a recent booklet,[1] offers the Church a programme based on such total commitment to mission. He exhorts us to recognise God's present warfare on a whole series of ills and injustices. We must 'identify the battles God is engaged in and read their development as prophetically as possible', because 'we are called to fight at the side of Jesus Christ in the power of the Holy Spirit till sin and evil are routed. *This is what is basic to the life of the Church.*'[2] He calls the Church to engage in the social and political and economic development of the nation. Task forces of technologists and economists (albeit, with a theological training) are to be set up 'to identify the battles God is engaged in'. The whole booklet is as spiritual as a government white paper. Faced with such brisk managerial optimism, today's flower children, in their search for what Augustine described as that beauty which was so ancient and so new, reasonably turn not to the Church but to Eastern religions and hallucinogenic drugs. The mystic would feel as much at home in the Church of today as he would at the Council for Increased Productivity.

The thing that dismays me about the wave of aggressive secularity in the Church is not its political correctness or wrongness. Christians have as much right as anyone to engage in political and social action, and they may even feel specifically obligated to do so. No, the dismaying thing is the failure to recognise the real needs of man, his profound hunger not as economic man, or technological man, or modern secular man, but simply as man; man thrust out into the cold of a profound cosmic loneliness. All men, said Ranke, are equidistant from eternity.[3] At the very heart of his humanity man has no new needs, only the old, old need for the living God.

4

The Flight from Transcendence

SO FAR I have attempted to describe a basic tension in the life of the Church: the tension between worship and mission. By worship I mean the response of the Church to the revelation of God in Christ by adoring self-offering. By mission I mean the spreading of the news of that revelation among all men. The Church's role of worship can lead to locking the revelation into an ecclesiastical ghetto where the message is preserved and celebrated. With the process of ghetto-isation, the missionary impulse is diminished and the gospel is foreshortened. On the other hand, in the face of a hostile culture, whose dominant assumptions are those of the cultured despiser of religion, the man of faith can consciously or unconsciously lose his nerve concerning the truth of his message and subtly surrender its distinctiveness. At first the surrender may be semantic: the vocabulary of faith is used merely as a code to describe attitudes and aspirations approved by the culture. Thus can substantive atheism be conjoined to a religious vocabulary, as, for instance, during the brief flowering of the movement in the USA called the gospel of Christian atheism. At its most honest, however, surrender can finally lead to an actual forsaking of the Christian message for the dominant cultural view of the day, a process the sociologists call 'going native'. I argued in chapters 2 & 3 that much of the theology of the 60s was a theology of surrender, an almost slavish attempt to adapt Christian faith to the culture of the 60s, at almost any cost.

Much of the attempt was very well intended. It was frequently a serious attempt to fulfil the command to spread the message among all men. The goal, however, is impossible: part of the attempt was simply wrongheaded and part of it was based on a mistaken interpretation of Matthew 28.19: 'Go, therefore, make disciples of all the nations.' Karl Barth has said 'nations' means people from among all nations. In other words, the Church is to be a representative community drawn from among the nations. Even more, the numerical fallacy, as we have called it, is not only a mistaken exegesis. It reflects a mistaken idea of the Church itself.

One of the dominant schools of thought in modern protestant theology has been called 'theological positivism', and it is usually associated with the early work of Karl Barth. It makes a profoundly pessimistic assessment of man. Man is utterly gone from righteousness, the image of God in his soul is utterly defaced. He inhabits spiritual darkness. He is powerless to reach God by his own efforts. There is, therefore, no natural knowledge of God at all. All the religious striving of man is a splendid illusion or, worse, arrogance and idolatry. Man is utterly shut up in prison. God's original creation is utterly corrupted. What can save man? Only an absolutely unilateral intrusion of God's grace. God's revelation and salvation suddenly appear as a vastly unmerited gift. Only the revelation from above contains the truth and the power of salvation. There is no other salvation. Only in the Incarnation, Death, and Resurrection of Christ is there salvation. There is no 'natural' grace. Only in the totality of the saving event can man find union with God.

There are certain obvious consequences to be drawn from such a dramatic theology, and among them are some positive merits. First of all, theological positivism lays important stress on the grace and power of God. Man's creation and sustaining *is* the work of God, an impelling fact that stands in permanent judgement on all man's arrogance and idolatry. The basic and primary fact of all religion is the glorious transcendence of God. It is the primary datum of faith. To the eternal credit of Karl Barth he dragged modern theology back to recognise that fact when it had surrendered to an anaemic liberalism unable to stand up against the demonic totalitarianism which stalked Europe in the twentieth century. Second, such theology does justice to the effectiveness of God's work in Christ. It rescues our concept of Christ from being purely subjective and sentimental. It defiantly opposes any reduction of the fundamental objectivity of the gospel events, and spurns any attempt to adjust the Christian faith to the dominant assumptions of the age. The revelation stands in judgement on all culture, and not the other way round.

Those are massive gains and although such theology has suffered an eclipse, history will judge it as an abiding contribution to the defence of the faith. Nevertheless, it has had several less desirable aspects.

In the first place, it implies a radical discontinuity between creation and redemption. It is important that we are God's by creation as well as by redemption; indeed, creation seems to be our primary relationship to God. The Bible says that God's creation, while disordered by man's sin, still lives in covenant with God.

> God spoke to Noah and to his sons with him: 'I now make my covenant with you and with your descendants after you, and with every living creature that is with you, all birds and cattle, all the wild animals with you on earth, all that have come out of the ark. I will make my covenant with you: never again shall all living creatures be destroyed by the waters of the flood, never again shall there be a flood to lay waste the earth'.
>
> God said, 'This is the sign of the covenant which I establish between myself and you and every living creature with you, to endless generations:
>
> > My bow I set in the cloud,
> > sign of the covenant
> > between myself and earth.
> > When I cloud the sky over the earth,
> > the bow shall be seen in the cloud.

Then I will remember the covenant which I have made between myself and you and living things of every kind.' (Genesis 9.8–15)

The covenant with Noah is the primary covenant between God and his creation. It establishes his relationship with 'living things of every kind'. Later covenants between God and particular peoples have meaning only within the larger and earlier covenant. Moreover, the later elections were calls to witness to all men concerning the primary reality of the world's relation to God. All subsequent covenants recall men to their relationship with God *by creation*. It is true that each covenanted people, whether Jew or Christian, has tended to take an exclusive view of its covenant, but always exclusiveness has been a profound and tragic mistake: the later covenants were representative, vicarious covenants on behalf of all men.

Man's primary relationship to God by creation is already a relationship, though unconsciously, in Christ. While Jesus Christ is the *concrete historical* revelation of God's presence and action in the world, he stands in continuity with God's action in the world from the beginning. The great events of the Old Testament as well as all genuine knowledge of God wherever it might be found are all of a piece with God's revelation in Christ, for

He is the image of the unseen God
and the first-born of all creation,
for in him were created

all things in heaven and on earth:
everything visible and everything invisible,
Thrones, Domination, Sovereignties, Powers—
all things were created through him and for him.
Before anything was created, he existed,
and he holds all things in unity. (Colossians 1.15-17)

Such knowledge liberates us from all exclusivist interpretations of Christian faith. E. Schillebeeckx, developing the same thought writes,

> the present universal order of existence is a supernatural order. Man is created for Christ (Colossians 1.16); no fully human moral orientation is possible without immediately being implicitly an orientation for or against the *Deus salutaris*. A religion founded purely on philosophical insight, 'mature religion' based on that which the unaided human spirit can achieve of itself, is a fiction, metaphysically impossible in fact, because the *eidos* of religion . . . necessarily implies personal relations between God and man, and these clearly cannot be achieved by the created powers of man alone.
>
> In the concrete, all religion presupposes an at least anonymous supernatural revelation and faith. There is thus, anterior to any Judeo-Christian religion, an *instinctus divinus* arising from the deepest foundations of human religious psychology as influenced by the attraction of divine grace.[1]

Such a view does not contradict the claim of theological positivism that all faith is of grace, but it does immensely widen the scope of grace to include the whole created order and man in all his religious strivings. Christianity's modern encounters with other religions has forced upon us the thrilling and

33

revolutionary idea that Christ is present in all religious faiths as the Word of God in its encounter with man. The positivistic attempt to cut off knowledge of and relationship with God by a narrow and fundamentalist interpretation of Jesus Christ has no warrant in scripture and contradicts the experience of mankind. Eugene Hillman has said, 'There are found in the various non-Christian religions certain valid fore-shadowings and fragments which, used by God in communicating the life of grace, constitute an "unconscious Christianity", recognised even by the early Fathers.' He goes on,

> St Augustine explains in a masterly manner how the service of God which we know and practise in the Church is as old as the world. He has divided the gradual coming into being of the Church in the course of human history into three great phases: the 'Church' of the devout heathen; the pre-Christian phase of the Christian Church in the form of the chosen race of Israel; and finally the emergence of the mature Church, the 'Church of the first-born'.
>
> In a nebulous but nonetheless discernible fashion the sacramental Church is already present in the life of the whole of mankind. All humanity receives that inward word of God calling men to a union of grace with himself. . .[2]

We must examine the Church's role in the world in a later section, but here it is important to note that one of the results of the positivistic rejection of the universalist note in biblical faith has led us to the theological impasse of the present day. In the first place, the positivist climate in religion led to a contempt for all 'natural religion', and a repudiation of all non-Christian faiths as having no point of continuity with Christianity. The effect on Western religion was two-fold. As the Western religious tradition wilted under the assault of radical secularism, it could not appeal for support to the religious experience of mankind. Contempt for 'natural theology' led in time to the curious flight from theology itself in much of the writing of the 60s. Some theologians have reached the ultimate paradox of a 'Jesus religion', but a Jesus cut off from the Father. In fact, a purely vertical inter-pretation of God's revelation in Christ has proved impossible to support without reference to God's presence in creation. Certain theologians have been left with little more than a nostalgic regard for Jesus and a touching faith that Western secularism has inherited the best of the Judeo-Christian tradition.

Thus theological positivism has had a most para-doxical effect on theology and the Church. It started as a movement to defend and proclaim the sovereign transcendence of God, but by disallowing any com-munion with or knowledge of God through the natural creation and by insisting on its own positivist account of the Revelation in Christ, it has removed the continuity between the explicit faith of Christianity and the faith implicit in the created order. Dialogue between Church and world became impossible. The Church was left defiantly proclaiming to the world a Revelation which the world had no way of understanding, since it implied not a fulfilment but a rejection of man's natural religious striving.

John MacQuarrie has described the whole process in a recent article on theology.

Karl Barth had come upon the scene after the First World War, protesting against the shallowness of the old liberal theology which, he believed, had its share of blame for the condition into which Europe had fallen. This liberal theology, he claimed, had domesticated God and made him the servant of human aspirations, a kind of patron saint to lend glamour to what men had already decided for themselves. As against all this, Barth stressed anew the transcendence and the sovereignty of God, and about this one may say, 'So far, so good'. But Barth thought that he could do this only by isolating the knowledge of God from everything else. He would allow no natural theology, no truth in the non-Christian religions, no universal sense of the presence of God, nothing outside of the specific biblical revelation.

Now, so long as that revelation stood, Barth did indeed have a ground of objectivity, and certainly he himself could not be accused of an excessive subjectivism. But if anyone ever began to have doubts about the validity of the revelation, then there was no possibility of supporting it by a reasoned apologetic, for natural theology and philosophy had been ruled out. It is not really surprising then to find that the most extreme exponents of a thorough-going subjectivism in contemporary Christian thought are almost all disillusioned Barthians. When the whole rational substructure of theology has been swept away and only the arbitrary appeal to revelation is left, then if ever a doubt arises about this revelation, there is no way left of dealing with it. Men like Gabriel Vahanian, Paul van Buren and William Hamilton who talk of the death of God and have moved very close to an atheistic position, came to that position through the theology of Karl Barth. Finding themselves deprived of any objective grounds for belief, they have to construct a purely subjective faith of their own which dispenses with God though it still leaves a residual role for Christ as a convenient figure who makes concrete our human moral ideals.[3]

Such a dramatic reduction of the gospel must have far-reaching effects on the Church's understanding of itself and its missionary role.

Perhaps the Church's growing reluctance to talk of God at all to the world, except with embarrassed modifications, has been a consequence. Theology in the 60s was often almost neurotically anxious not to be unworldly, or shackled to a transcendent God, evidenced in the rather self-conscious attempts of the clergy to swing in time with the cultural pendulum. There was a massive role crisis, and many were no longer able to remain in the ministry. The Christian ministry must find its purpose, if any, in spiritual categories. Evelyn Underhill, saw the problem long ago,

We are drifting towards a religion which consciously or unconsciously keeps its eye on humanity rather than on Deity—which lays all the stress on service and hardly any of the stress on awe: and that is a type of religion which in practice does not wear well. It does little for the soul in those awful moments when the pain and mystery of life are most deeply felt. It does not provide a place for that profound experience which Tauler calls 'suffering in God'. It does not lead to sanctity: and sanctity after all is the religious goal. It does not fit those who accept it as adequate for the solemn privilege of guiding souls to God. . . . In fact it turns its back on the most profound gifts made by Christianity to the human race. I do not think we can deny that there is . . . a definite trend in the direction of religion of this shallow social type. . . . It will only be checked insofar as the clergy are themselves real men of prayer. Therefore to become and continue a real man of prayer, seems to me the first duty of a parish priest. What is a man of prayer? He is one who deliberately wills and steadily desires that his intercourse with God and other souls shall be controlled and actuated at every point by God himself; one who has so far developed and educated his spiritual sense that his supernatural environment is more real and solid than his natural environment. This is . . . a description of the only real apostolic life. The laity distinguish in a moment [members of] the clergy who have it from [those] who have it not: there is nothing you can do for God or for the souls of men which exceeds in importance the achievement of that spiritual temper and attitude.[4]

If a priest loses his grasp of supernatural reality, if he is no longer able to have his ministry validated only in the eyes of God and his Church, what is he to do? In our pragmatic and empirical culture, he must seek some external validation for his role. He will move more and more into a life-style of good works in an attempt to attain merit, Pelagian-style. As his unease with his own role grows, however, and his filial contempt for the Church increases, he is liable to move right out of the ministry into one of the serving professions, such as teaching or social work. If he is able, he may gravitate to some faculty of theology or other, where he'll flay the fat Christian with Savanarolan glee.

Such are the consequences of the tragic repudiation of what is loosely described as 'natural theology', the conviction that God has been graciously active in his creation from the beginning until now, drawing men to him 'in diverse, fragmentary manners'. The Church can recover her nerve only when she becomes aware again that God's saving grace has preceded her in any situation, even in the defiantly secularist milieu of the West.

> The grace of God has always been there ahead of our preaching; a man is always in a true sense a Christian already when we begin to commend Christianity to him. For he is a man already included in God's general will for salvation, redeemed by Christ, with grace already living and working in his innermost heart at least as the preferred possibility of supernatural action. . . . Any communication of Christianity is always a communication of what is already there, alive, within a man. . . . It is on this supposition that we can hope that there are many who are Christians without explicitly knowing it, that grace is more widely accepted than is recorded in the Church's statistics. . . .[5]

As we have seen, the relaxed confidence, that the Christian Gospel was at home in its Father's world, deserted much Protestant theology in the 60s producing a fascinating if tragic theological complex.

Eugene Hillman states very clearly what is the true meaning of the Church's missionary task

> The accomplishment of the missionary function among the nations is a conditional *sign* of the end. The presence of the Church among the nations is a sacramental, and therefore

39

symbolic, sign which tangibly signifies an invisible reality. Precisely because it is a symbolic sign, its validity does not depend on the total conversion to the visible Church of every single individual in one place; for only a few are chosen to stand for all among their own people.[6]

If, however, the Christian gospel comes completely from outside history, if the image of God is defaced in man utterly and man has no 'natural' knowledge of God, if God's grace is not at work in his creation apart from the conscious work of the Christian community, it follows that a man's salvation depends upon his explicit acceptance of the Christian revelation. This means that the Church is not a priestly sign in the world, existing for and on behalf of the whole world. Instead, she is an ark floating upon the waters of destruction, pulling men aboard, since there can be no salvation apart from her.

By a tragic inversion, however, such theological positivism was unable to sustain itself in the face of radical secularism. She had no philosophical tools, only a defiant certainty which became less and less certain. The whole paradoxical conclusion was summed up in the title of a book review in the *Christian Century* some time ago: 'God is dead and Jesus is his Son.'

The purpose was commendable. The Church, it was believed, could now be liberated for real involvement with the world. The cross was beaten into a sword and the theologian went forth to join the revolution.

Except that, as Evelyn Underhill pointed out, in practice, a religion which lays all its stress on service and hardly any on awe does not wear well. 'It does little for the soul in those awful moments when the pain and mystery of life are most deeply felt.' Already we may hope, the waters are beginning to clear.

5

The Publicity Syndrome

It is possible to discern some order in this multiplicity, to stop the dialogue, as it were, at certain points; and to define typical partial answers that recur so often in different eras and societies that they seem to be less the product of historical conditioning than of the nature of the problem itself and the meaning of its terms—Richard Niebuhr[1]

IN THIS book I have been discussing the tension in the life of the Church between worship and mission—worship, the Church in its relation to God; and mission, the Church's relation to the world. I have argued that the temptation to the Church at worship is to become a kind of ghetto, walling out disturbing doubts and distractions, and that the temptation to the Church as mission is to surrender its distinctive message in order to appeal to greater numbers of men. The terms, however, are not really antithetic. It is arguable that what I have called ghetto can be a form of surrender.

The great orthodox churches of the east, are worshipping communities that have allowed the missionary imperative to atrophy by locking it into the lectionary of divine worship. They are churches of the ghetto; but, is not their isolation a particular kind of surrender? Have they not simply acquiesced in the cultural role assigned to them by their societies? Was not Marx correct in saying that such religion is a drug, a surrendered Christianity which fortifies the dominant political ideology of the day? Had it not become part of the exploiting apparatus which enabled the rich man to sit in his castle while the poor man was at his gate? Perhaps the ghetto is the most dangerous form of surrender, because its preoccupation with the divine mystery disguises from itself how well it has been taken in by the State. It seems to be true today of the Roman Catholic Church in Spain, Portugal, and South America and of the Dutch Reformed Church in South Africa. The true tension, then, may not be between ghetto and surrender, but between faithfulness and unfaithfulness. In any event, I am moving in this book towards such a view. I am not about to enunciate a water-tight set of theological categories, but am merely searching for a rudimentary tool which will enable us to locate where we are at the moment. In Niebuhr's words, partial answers are 'less the product of historical conditioning than of the nature of the problem itself and the meaning of its terms'.

The same sort of polarity occurs in politics. Right or left wing are the customary responses to political problems, and the fact that extreme right-wing politics is in its results uncannily like extreme left-wing politics, should not surprise us.

One may add a note which seems relevant on the paradox of change—change that always defeats itself because it cannot stop: once admitted, one change produces the wish for another *ad infinitum* and it is Chronus eating his children. The opponents of change at the same time produce what they most wish to avoid, an almost identical result by explosion as it were, trying to bottle people up in what is abhorrent to nature—a *status quo*: the changers destroy because they are rootless, and the conservers keep because they fear: between them the transmitter, or transformer, alters if he can without destroying, and makes a habitable world, not overstraining. It is a mistake to think of extreme left and right as opposite when their results are so often the same: the true contrast is between either of them and the moderates, who, whether they belong to one side or the other, resemble each other in their effects and have, incidentally, been for many centuries the strength and fortune of policy in England—builders and not destroyers. This is why it seems to me that a choice between a reasonable subverter and an adventurous conservative is a matter of small importance, whereas the choice between these two and either extreme is full of risk and danger.[2]

The Church exists in a similar tension. There have been right-wing responses to the problems of its relation with the world and there have been left-wing responses. Ghetto and surrender are antithetic in this way: neither can have the only word. The most fashionable voice in theology during the last decade, however, has been that of the left-wing. One reason has been the highly sensational nature of much of the theology of the 60s.

Communication is one of the vogue words of our time. There is a kind of communication explosion.

Never before in history have so few men been engaged in communicating so little to so many. The communications men have become the mandarins of our era. The media bring their apparently effortless omniscience into our homes, simplifying and encapsulating everything. They demand the quick answer as they abhor the reflective pause. Everything tends to be reduced to a slick and easily remembered formula. Daniel Boorstin has said,

> The nature of both TV and radio is that they abhor silence and 'dead time'. All TV and radio discussion programmes are compelled to snap question and answer back and forth as if the contestants were adversaries in an intellectual match. Although every experienced newspaperman and inquirer knows that the most thoughtful and responsive answers to any difficult question come after a long pause, and that the longer the pause the more illuminating the thought that follows it, none the less the electronic media cannot bear to suffer a pause of more than five seconds: a pause of thirty seconds of dead time on air seems interminable.[3]

Whatever the ultimate effect of the communication explosion on our culture, certain trends are easily detectable. In the first place, the media themselves create events, either directly, by setting up pseudo-events which are then recorded; or indirectly, by offering individuals or groups with a need or desire for publicity an opportunity to fabricate publicisable events. In the second place, the media sets the style of events by consciously or unconsciously influencing public figures to speak in highly quotable excerpts. It produces celebrity folk-figures 'known for their well-knownness', who can, at a moment's notice, make a particular event important, who can make instant copy. Their style, whether consciously or unconsciously, conforms to the demands and limitations of the media. Whether a pop-singer, a radical bishop or an academic, the celebrity can be relied on to create the appropriate titillation on the correct wave-band. In such a culture, who can tell what is unreal, when the real criterion is no longer intrinsic significance but publicity value?

An example of the process is the episcopal career of John Robinson. His little book *Honest to God* was a highly publicisable event appropriate to the dynamics of the communications media. There is little news value when a book is published which appears to advocate a kind of agnosticism, however safely it hedges its final bets. When, however, the author is a bishop, who seems to be saying something outrageous, then the publication of the book itself becomes highly noticeable. Book + bishop + the needs of the media = event. I am not suggesting that Robinson manipulated the media to sell his own books or project his own personality. On the contrary, he has been manipulated by the media and used by them. He has become a *news event*. He has come to be reported because he makes good reporting, and not because of the intrinsic value of what he has to say. His views on God, sex, and Playboy magazine would be non-events if attributed to a garage proprietor in Nottingham, but John Robinson makes them news. Robinson belongs, not to the theology but to the cultural anthropology of the 60s.

The electronic, news-oriented culture of the 60s has exerted an enormous influence on theology and the Churches. The modern appetite for the new (called *neophilia* in a perceptive book by Christopher Booker) has produced a bewildering flow of theological and religious fads. The decade opened, propitiously, with Penguin Books' publication of *Lady Chatterley's Lover*. In the court case that followed, Bishop Robinson delighted the front pages of the world by describing the adulterous relationship between Mellors and Lady Chatterley as 'essentially sacred . . . as in a real sense an act of holy communion'. Pronounced with utmost solemnity in the voice we were to hear so often, with no hint of conscious humour behind the preposterous words, the whole episode was comic.

The whole decade flashes across my mind like some lunatic kaleidoscope: the Rector of Woolwich pushing a beauty queen through the streets in a wheel barrow; Malcolm Boyd going on TV to announce with passionate solemnity that Jesus Christ, like all men, had a penis; Canon Montefiore of Cambridge electrifying the world press by saying that Jesus Christ could have been a homosexual; an up-to-date harvest festival in the South of England in which the liturgy had been written by the vicar, ending with the following responsory: 'Are we happy? You bet your life we're happy!' Appropriately, the 60s ended with another awe-struck pronouncement from John Robinson. In the pages of the *Sunday Times* he breathlessly intoned: 'The August issue of Playboy . . . contains some marvellous cine-photographic stills of Paula Kelly dancing completely in the nude, pubic hair and all. Nothing could have been more beautiful and entrancing.' Ah, the 60s!

There were more sombre episodes, of course. One of them, as noted, was the steady trickle of men leaving the ministry for teaching and social work. But there was a certain irony, for were they not leaving the Church because, in the rhetoric of the day, they found the structures of the Church (mystic phrase!) 'irrelevant to the needs of the world'? And to whom did they go? Why, to educational and social work agencies, to structures of almost Byzantine complexity! Having strained at the ecclesiastical gnat, they swallowed the societal camel!

Above all, theology was affected. An influential school of theologians announced the death of God, with scarcely a smile, and one of them went so far as to provide an approximate date for the demise of the deity. Trendy clerics took the signal to turn their sanctuaries into coffee houses and their confessionals into couches, and much of the Church embarked upon an orgy of self-mutilation almost obscene in its intensity. The epitaph for the whole theological decade was offered by the Reverend Mr Mackerel in Peter De Vries' *Mackerel Plaza:* 'The final proof of God's Omnipotence is that he does not need to exist in order to save us.' Ah, the 60s!

My whole ministry has been spent in the 60s. The 60s formed me. You might say that the 60s corrupted me. As I look back on the decade I see that it led me and many in the Church on a theological detour. The medium became the message, in McLuhanese. Today's theologians are so intent on translating the message into a medium of communication which the world will understand that they have allowed the language to replace the reality it was meant to convey. The medium has usurped the message, the style has replaced the substance—an apt comment on the weird unreality in which we live. The modern public relations industry has created a situation in which image has become more important than substance, the sell more important than the thing sold. By the time he has captured the public's ear, the jet-age theologian often has nothing left to say to them that they don't already know. In an age when language has been devalued by the pedlars of instant unreality, it may be a time for theologians to keep their distance and their soul while they

> Strive to recast once more
> That attar of the ore
> In the strong mould of pain
> Till it is whole again. . . .

49

Is it possible to say today what the Church, God help it, stands in history as a witness to? What follows in this book is a very personal and possibly foolhardy attempt to do so. Contrary to much of the fashionable theology of the last decade, it seems to me that man's experience of life does point to and prepare for God's revelation in Christ. God has been active in his creation from the beginning, drawing men to him in many and different ways. Such natural longings are not the work of man: they are the promptings of God, if we will but seek after him and find him. They are not lacking in the lives of so-called religionless secular man. It seems to me that there are at least three areas in life which prompt man towards a recognition of the transcendence of God—what Peter Berger might call 'rumours' of God left in his creation. The first is man's compulsion to understand himself and the whole of life. The second is man's longing for stability in a world of change and decay. And the third is man's strange sense that death, the most natural of processes, is profoundly contradictory to his deepest intuitions. Those three experiences, it seems to me, are signals of transcendence to man, that may lead him to the fullness of God's self-revelation in Christ.

PART TWO

6

Man's Search for Understanding

SOME YEARS ago an unusual news item appeared in English newspapers. A boxer called Ronnie van der Walt had been one of the golden boys of South African boxing. He was tough, he was willing, and he was white. He had knocked out a contender for the world welter-weight title and he seemed to be on his way to the top. Then one night, just before he was to fight another white South African boxer, his name was inked out of the programme, and posters with his picture were stripped off walls. 'If he'd fought that night,' said the promoter, 'he would have been fined or gone to jail.' Ronnie had come to the end of his boxing career. The reason? The government had pronounced him 'coloured,' a person of mixed blood, and therefore unfit to fight in the ring with white men. As Ronnie recalled it: 'The inspector walked around us peering at us from every angle like you do when you buy an animal. He said nothing, just looked.' Soon Ronnie got a letter telling him that at 29 years he had been reclassified as coloured. That meant he could no longer box for a living. He could no longer live in a white neighbourhood or send his children to a white school. His life had been torn up at the roots. His protests were useless. After proudly pointing out that he was the grandson of Johannes van der Walt, a great Afrikaans wrestler, he added: 'They can't just cut me down like a bloody tree. For God's sake, I am a man.' But they did. They cut him down like a bloody tree. In one rugged and despairing line of poetry Ronnie van der Walt expressed the pathos and greatness of man: 'They can't just cut me down like a bloody tree. For God's sake, I am a man.'

Ronnie van der Walt's tragedy, which in essence is the whole tragedy of South Africa, is that the government had denied his fundamental humanity. What *is* a man? According to Eric Fromm the thing that characterises man as man is the freedom to create his own destiny. In the account of man given in Genesis, man is seen as being created in God's likeness with a capacity for an evolution of which the limits are not set. 'God,' says a Hasidic Master, 'does not say that "it was good" after creating man; that indicates that while the cattle and everything else were finished after being created, man was not finished.'[1]

Unlike the rest of nature man is an open system, not a fixed system. In other words 'the human' is not a static, fixed essence; it is a dynamic category. Man as man is an evolving being in constant process of becoming what he is destined to be. To be 'fully human' is not to have a given set of natural characteristics, but to be on a journey, to be involved in a constant effort of self-transcendence. Man is character-ised, above all, by freedom.

Compare man, 'the open system', with another part of creation which is a 'closed system', such as a tree. A tree, unlike man, has a fixed fate. Its fate is to reach its glory, to wither, and to die. The glory that the tree reaches is 'fate'. It is not anything that the tree itself accomplishes. It is an effortless process of nature. We talk, poetically, of trees battling the elements, but we don't mean it. Trees, unlike men, do not battle. They are part of the unconscious fecun-dity of nature. Man is different. The glory that dis-tinguishes man from nature is the dreadful freedom to create his own future, to discover his own destiny. Unlike the tree whose essential nature and purpose is given ineluctably with its existence, man's essential nature and purpose are for him to create, to quarry out of history by his own efforts. Man is a creature, not of fate, but of destiny.

His need to battle for the meaning of his own life presents man with several overwhelming problems. The most basic is the difficulty of understanding his own existence, the problem of knowledge. John Hick's study *Evil and the God of Love*, offers a novel approach to the traditional thesis that God's purpose for man is to love him and be loved by him. Hick notes first that for God's end to be achieved, man must be endowed with a certain relative autonomy. Man must be set at a certain distance from his

Creator. How can anything be set at a distance from God?

> The kind of distance between God and man that would make room for a degree of human autonomy is epistemic distance. (*A gap of knowledge.*) In other words, the reality and presence of God must not be borne in upon men in the coercive way in which their natural environment forces itself upon their attention. The world must be to man, to some extent at least, *as though there was no God*. God must be knowable but only by a mode of knowledge that involves a *free personal response* on man's part, this response consisting in an uncompelled interpretative activity whereby we experience the world as mediating the divine presence.[2]

The concept of the epistemic distance between God and man is profoundly important. It means that *the world* is the primary object of man's knowledge and concern. More importantly, it means that God's presence is mediated by the world *as we try to interpret its meaning*. Hick identifies man's cognitive freedom from God with the Fall:

> The creation of man in his own relatively autonomous world, in which he is cognitively free in relation to his Maker, is what mythological language calls the Fall of Man. . . . Man exists at a distance from God's goal for him, however, not because he has fallen from that goal but because he has yet to arrive at it.[3]

So great is the freedom of man that it extends even to his knowledge of God. God *is* knowable, 'but only by a mode of knowledge that involves a free personal response on man's part'.[4]

Man then is created 'an open system'. His future is 'possibility', the achievement of his own destiny. Moreover, the world is given to man as the primary reality. The reality of the world is also 'possibility' because it does not yield its meaning and secret without drama and suffering. Here, too, man is committed to a search and a struggle. This is the meaning of the myth of the Fall: the investigation, control and interpretation of the world. The creative exercise of freedom leads man to experience the world as mediating the divine presence.

How does it happen?

As man exercises his freedom he interprets his experience in formal ways, such as science and morality and history. The paradoxical discovery he makes is the ultimate uncertainty in his attitude to the world. Schubert Ogden calls it the phenomenon of 'the limiting question.' If man pursues his inquiries he reaches those limiting questions to which his experience of the world affords no answer. Ogden maintains that such questions can be given only what he calls 'religious answers'. The alternative is endless reiteration or the endless cataloguing of particular instances, neither of which affords a satisfying answer to basic questions about human existence.

Ogden maintains that all of man's 'interpretative activities', to use Hick's phrase, finally point beyond themselves. His explanation is the phrase already noted: 'the limiting question.' Sometimes the chain of moral reasoning, for example, leads back to a limiting question to which no moral answer can be given: Why do anything moral at all? To that question no *moral* reasoning can give an answer. Yet it is precisely the question raised by our existence. We meet the same kind of limiting questions at the boundaries of science, questions that betray a fundamentally natural uncertainty on the part of man as he faces what frequently appears to be the meaningless immensity of life.

E. L. Mascall deals with the problem with characteristic dispatch. He says that it is reasonable to suppose that if you begin from this world in the way we have been describing, you must go beyond it if you are to get anywhere at all. He quotes Dr C. B. Daly:

If my empirical knowledge forces me to ask questions which cannot be answered in empirical terms, then I know that empirical knowledge is not adequate to the reality which I am. But to know that knowledge is inadequate is a valid and a most important kind of knowledge. It is a perpetual invitation to deeper reflection; but also an awareness that reflection will never come to an end of what there is to know. . . .

Metaphysics begins with the recognition that there is mystery in being and in experience. But it is not merely the recognition of mystery. Metaphysics cannot end until it has rendered such reason of that mystery that it shall not become instead absurdity. The true alternative is not mystery *or* clarity, but mystery *or* absurdity.[5]

Our real problem, the problem that lies always under the surface of our lives, is to accept ourselves and the world despite the threat to meaning posed by finitude and death. Men are moved by a deep desire for reassurance, for a general confidence about the future, and so there arises the limiting questions to give that desire explicit expression.[6] The important word here is reassurance.

At this point Ogden's argument takes an interesting twist. Man is not engaged in putting hypothetical answers to theoretical questions. The answers provided by what Ogden calls 'religious discourse' are not new to man; they are not experienced as something utterly novel presented from outside. In fact, man recognises the answers as corresponding to an assurance which he already has, a sort of ineradicable confidence in the meaning of life and the ultimate significance of his own actions. Ogden maintains that the undergirding confidence, which is the experience of the presence of God in the actualities of life, is what informs all of man's morality, or purposefulness of any sort. His remarks about Camus are illuminating.

According to Camus, life is essentially absurd. We must live without any guarantee that our own actions are finally worthwhile. Nevertheless, the only fitting response to the absurdity is a heroic revolt and an affirmation of life which comes, in Camus, to embrace a profoundly humanistic ethic of love. That position is intriguing, says Ogden, but it can hardly define a real possibility, whether for thought or for real choice. His argument is important.

> If all our actions are, in principle, absurd, the act of heroically resisting their absurdity must also be absurd. It, too, is *ex hypothesi* a totally meaningless response and can be supposed not a bit more fitting than the various attempts to flee from absurdity that Camus so unsparingly condemns. Or, to take the other side of the dilemma, insofar as resistance for the sake of man *is* a meaningful act—is somehow fitting as the alternatives to it are not—the absurdity of our existence cannot be as unrelieved as was originally alleged.[7]

There is evidence that Camus was aware of his inconsistency, and many have seen in his thought a genuine religious faith. Ogden argues from such evidence that, implicit in any purposeful human activity like morality or science, necessarily resides an underlying confidence in life's meaning, a confidence in a reality transcending the natural reality experienced in the world. The *limiting question* exposes the world's inability to explain itself by itself. We are always brought to a frontier, a boundary in our knowledge, where the answer has to come from outside. Yet the answer, we discover, is not from outside; it was already within us as a conviction that undergirded all the small and large purposes of our life. We have travelled far to find what was before us all along.

> And where was I when I was seeking thee? There thou wast, before me; but I had gone away, even from myself, and I could not find myself, much less thee.[8]

60

Nevertheless, this natural trust has to become reflective belief. We can say three things about reflective belief.

1. It makes explicit that implicit confidence in life which is the ground and motive of all our purposeful activity.
2. It makes reflective and intelligible what is intuitive and unspoken.
3. It vividly and radically affirms what you really *are* and will henceforth dedicate yourself to *be*.

This 'making real' of faith is crucial for man because man is so constituted that, unless he realises who he is and in whom he trusts, he is in constant danger of binding himself to 'them that are no gods'. G. K. Chesterton once remarked that when men cease to believe in a god, they do not then believe in nothing but in anything. It is important for men to know the reality that lies behind all their unspoken longing, the one reality to which the Church witnesses. If they don't they end by worshipping anything.

Whom therefore ye ignorantly worship, him declare I unto you . . . For in him we live and move and have our being. (Acts 17.21)

7

Man's Search

IN CHAPTER 6 we discussed the question of man's knowledge of himself and the world. If man pushes the quest of knowledge and understanding to the limit he reaches a boundary, a 'limiting question' which demands a solution from outside. The epistemological search ends with a leap towards transcendence. The same is true of man's experience of life. Man's life is filled with a strange passion for fulfilment accompanied by a mysterious sense of loss. His experience of life points beyond life. The tragic sense of incompleteness is not something we can theorise about. It can really only be expressed in poem and parable. Everyman has known experiences that illumine the whole human condition, little flashes of insight into his strange nature. One of the most evocative images for the nature of man is that of the pilgrim or traveller. There is something fundamentally unsettled about man; he is never completely at home in the universe. He constantly has dreams that outdistance his achievements, like Arthur Miller's salesman, Willy Loman, chained to a dream he can never fulfil:

Willy was a salesman. And for a salesman, there is no rock bottom to the life. He don't put a bolt to a nut, he don't tell you the law or give you medicine. He's a man way out there in the blue, riding on a smile and a shoeshine. And when they start not smiling back—that's an earthquake. And then you get yourself a couple of spots on your hat, and you're finished. Nobody dast blame this man. A salesman is got to dream, boy. It comes with the territory.[1]

We have all experienced that fundamental insecurity. 'There is no rock bottom to the life.' We may try to build or buy ourselves onto a rock, but we can't—for long. Certain places, certain experiences in life, can overpower us with a sense of vulnerability. One afternoon in New York City I was engulfed by an overwhelming sense of the transience and wistfulness of man. It came upon me with the power of a revelation as I was walking from Greenwich Village to the East Side. I crossed the Bowery and picked my way round and over the customary quota of bleary derelicts sprawled on the sidewalks in alcoholic oblivion. The Bowery always impresses me with its squalid honesty. It is the bottom. You can't fall any lower. There, after a bitter pilgrimage, each man has reached his gutter. Every city has its Bowery. The Boweries of the world fulfil an almost sacrificial function. The men of the Old Testament used to offer the first-fruits of all their crops to God, the finest grain, the most perfect beast. In our Boweries we offer to the City a sort of 'last fruits': the weak and the soiled and the derelict, the ones who never made it. A pilgrimage to the Bowery can be a salutory experience.

Then I turned into a surprisingly different little street that runs between the Bowery and Tompkins Square. The sidewalks were swept clean and the little shops and bars had an unmistakable foreignness about them. I could not quite place it, but I felt that I had found a little back-water of history. When I reached the end of the street I found the answer on a shop sign. It said: 'Ukrainian Bazaar.' In the shop window there were beautifully carved and painted hens sitting on clutches of painted eggs. There were holy pictures. There were pictures of peasant girls in Ukrainian costume. Everything looked as if it had been brought out after having been stored in someone's attic for half a century.

I moved on into Tompkins Square. The sense of time changed. The square was firmly and aggressively of our time. Concrete benches. Kids playing baseball. A few surviving hippies. Sitting in the midst of all, however, were hundreds of old Ukrainians: women in black with scarves round their heads and old men leaning on sticks. They talked hardly at all. They conveyed, behind those secret Slav faces, a sense of displacement. They didn't quite belong anywhere. They may have left Russia during the Revolution over fifty years ago. Yet they had never really left Holy Russia. The acute nostalgia of the Ukrainian Bazaar was witness to that. Maybe they had sons who lived in Queens and followed the ball games, but their own present had become a memorialising of the past. They'd gone looking for another country and found themselves as strangers and pilgrims on the earth. At that moment in Tompkins Square I had a vivid sense of the restlessness and transience of man, crisscrossing history with endless journeyings.

The search for another country seems to have been characteristic of man as long as history has known him. He is a creature on the move, endlessly searching. The journey takes many forms. Men are constantly leaving their own land to seek another and a better country. The Old Testament is the record of a pilgrim people, endlessly moving on to a Promised Land and endlessly failing to fulfil their search. Today the search is vertical rather than horizontal. Sociologists talk about the 'upward mobility' of Western man, as he mounts the ladder of consumer affluence. Today's journey, however, is impelled by the same restlessness and ends in the same dissatisfaction. We are conscious of a desire which no natural happiness seems able to satisfy. There seems to be a gap in our being and no amount of *things* will fill it.

Some men come to identify it with certain moments in the past and take refuge in a nostalgic archaism. It doesn't work. C. S. Lewis pointed out that if you did get back to those moments in the past you would not find the thing you were looking for:

The books or the music in which we thought the beauty was located will betray us if we trust to them; it was not *in* them, it only came *through* them, and what came through them was longing . . . they are not the thing itself; they are only the scent of a flower we have not found, the echo of a tune we have not heard, news from a country we have never yet visited.[2]

Another form of the search is the political journey, the search for a better society. One of the indelible passions of man is the search for the perfect society, utopia, the kingdom of Heaven on earth. Many of the best minds and noblest souls in history have given themselves to that search. Indeed, man's history is the history of that search. That search and that passion is the most characteristic feature of our own day. However disfigured and ugly the results, man seems engaged in an endless struggle to bring some great thing to pass, to batter some harmony out of the terrible discords of creation. There is in man a terrible kingdom-need, a hunger for what the Old Testament calls *shalom* and we weakly translate as peace. But *shalom* is a dynamic ideal; it is a total harmony of creation, a peace that passes all understanding. He is a poor man who has never felt the call of that ideal, who has never girded himself and gone out into the struggle. Indeed, he is no man at all, for it is that hunger for righteousness that marks us as men—and yet—we never quite bring in the Kingdom; we never quite find the Other Country. Frustrations and ambiguities soon take over every revolution.

Still, there are many men who never leave home and who never engage in revolutionary politics; but they too are on a journey. They look for a place to settle down in, a place where they can gather happiness and security around them, a place unspoiled by regret. Marriage and children is the commonest form of the search. Men try to root themselves in the security of the family. It becomes the Other Country—successfully, to a very great extent. There is nothing quite like the warmth of belonging to a family, the security of love—and yet, time passes and robs us of that, too. I often find myself watching my children at sleep or at play. There is an exquisite vulnerability about children. You wrap them in your own strength and you want time to stand still and contain you in that moment, in the country of love. Nevertheless one day your children must go on their own search for the Other Country. Their search may take them to the ends of the earth; it may take them deep into unhappiness or despair; and you can only stand by, powerless in love. No parent can escape the endless wistfulness that goes hand in hand with the joy that children bring. Nor does marriage provide everlasting security. There is the old enemy, Death, that cuts us off from our longing and leaves us to walk alone.

Man, then, is afflicted with a desire which no natural happiness will satisfy. We can never go back to where we were, and we never quite arrive at where we're going.

The voice said, Cry. And he said, What shall I cry? All flesh is grass, and all the goodliness thereof is as the flower of the field: the grass withereth, the flower fadeth. (Isaiah 40.6)

So man is brought to a strange frontier of desire—afflicted with a longing that wanders, uncertain of its object, seeking rest and finding none. As in the epistemological search, man's longing points beyond this life. Man is again faced with a leap towards transcendence. C. S. Lewis asks,

> Is there any reason to suppose that the universe offers any satisfaction to it? 'Nor does the being hungry prove that we have bread.' But I think it may be urged that this misses the point. A man's physical hunger does not prove that man will get any bread; he may die of starvation on a raft in the Atlantic. But surely a man's hunger does prove that he comes of a race which repairs its body by eating and inhabits a world where eatable substances exist. In the same way, though I do not believe that my desire for Paradise proves that I shall enjoy it, I think it a pretty good indication that such a place exists and that some men will. A man may love a woman and not win her; but it would be very odd if the phenomenon called 'falling in love' occurred in a sexless world.[3]

St Augustine maintained that the craving for the Other Country, for the perfect society, for a joyful security, is a sort of homing instinct in man. As a pigeon circles and circles over its loft before landing, so man restlessly searches about himself, wandering through country after country, searching for his resting place, catching glimpses of it, sometimes short sometimes long, but never, in this life, being fully at home. Only in God does he find that country that is his heart's desire.

As Augustine asks, where did the desire for happiness come from in man, the strange expectation that, somehow, we *ought* to be happy? He says that it comes from the memory. The Other Country is not a place we have never yet found our way to: it is a place we knew once but have forgotten how to return to. It remains in our memory, haunting us. We come from God; he is our Country, and our whole life, in all its forms, is a searching back towards him who is our peace. In the words of Augustine's prayer: 'O God, you have made us for yourself alone, and our heart is restless till it rests in you.' So it is not surprising that man is endlessly dissatisfied and disappointed with everything less than God, for nothing less than God will really fill his need. Only there is he complete.

> Let them cast themselves upon thee . . . after all their weary wanderings . . . where was I when I was seeking thee? There thou wast, before me; but I had gone away, even from myself, and I could not find myself, much less thee.[4]

The Christian Church witnesses to the one reality that lies behind all man's searching. It stands in history as a sign which reassures man, proclaiming that 'the desire of all nations has come'.

8

Death

FEBRUARY IS the three o'clock in the morning of the year. Hope is at its lowest ebb. A funeral in February is even more poignant than usual. One funeral in February exemplifies the feeling of total emptiness which I am trying to describe. A young couple whom I'd known for some years lost their only child, a baby, and we went from Glasgow down to a village outside Lanark to bury him in the family lair. Just a few of us on a bitter biting day. The tiny cemetery was on the slope of a hill streaked with snow. John insisted on carrying the tiny white coffin himself. He clutched it with a fierce loneliness and carried it to the little grave. We all stood round the hole and I threw earth onto the whiteness at the bottom and spoke words into the wind. Then we stood round and touched each other the way you have to when there are no words that will do. We got back into the big, black cars and the doors shut with wistful finality. As we drove back to the city I was engulfed with the pity of it all. Death should not be. It revolted my conscience. Something was wrong somewhere.

Death is a great problem for man. A recent

newspaper article described it as 'the great unmention-able'. On the face of it, it is strange that death should be such a problem, because it is the one certain fact of our existence. One day each of us will die. We are always old enough to die, and to be born is already to be on the way to death. Even if our own death seems unreal to us, we cannot avoid the presence of death all around us. Death and decay are part of the rhythm of life. Life is full of death. There are lots of little ways in which in the midst of life we are in death. The lonely figure watching the car disappear round the bend before turning in at the door. That moment when you can't say goodbye at the airport because your heart seems to be filling your throat and you clutch hands and turn away. Sometimes life seems to be an endless rehearsal for death: the passing of the seasons and the falling of leaves; children growing up and people dying—old men and young men, good men and bad, unknown and well-known, men who are mourned and men who leave no trace. There are moments when the contemplation of such things seems to take the spring out of life: the sense of waste and decay: the constant experience of change and chance: the fact that 'nothing continueth in one stay': the endless wistfulness of creation.

You know what they say: 'It takes nine months to create a man, and only a single day to destroy him.' We both of us have known the truth of this as well as any one could ever know it. . . . Listen, May: it does not take nine months to make a man, it takes fifty years—fifty years of sacrifice, of determination, of—so many things! And when that man has been achieved, when there is no childishness left in him, nor any adolescence, when he is truly, utterly, a man—the only thing he is good for is to die.[1]

Most men have felt something of Malraux's sense of personal futility in the face of the nullifying certainty of death. Despite our moments of hard-headed rationality in the face of death, it remains, for most men, if not a matter for fear or frustration, at least a matter for regret. Because of our sense of the absurdity of death a whole literature of protest has grown up on the subject. Indeed, the poetic gift often brings a raging concern with death.

> Do not go gentle into that good night
> Old age should burn and rage at close of day
> Rage, rage against the dying of the light.[2]

Is there an answer to the problem of death? Can we, in fact, 'go gentle into that good night' in trust, or must we rage impotently at the dying of the light? How can man deal with death?

It is not strange that man should experience radical unease in the face of death, for if death has no meaning then the whole of life is finally meaningless, what someone once called 'the tinkling prelude to unending silence'. As Ladislaus Boros has pointed out, the search for some content in life and some continuity in human existence has to start as an inquiry into the meaning of death.

We have to recognise, first of all, that, apart from the human feelings involved, death is a frightful necessity. If the living stopped dying, the world would become a monstrous place. If people stopped dying, in several generations there would not even be standing room on earth.

> To obviate the absolute necessity of death, the reproduction of living things would have had to cease soon after it began. The consequence of this would be the absence of all growth, all evolution of the species. Man, the result of a long evolutionary process, would never have appeared on earth, or, on the assumption that he was 'created' on the first day of the biosphere, would never have evolved to his present state. In a word, we can conceive of the absence of death only in an entirely static universe where a determined number of members of different species would have been created in the beginning and remained constant for the duration. I do not know whether such a universe would have been preferable to our own. But there is no doubt that in an evolutionary universe death is a necessity.[3]

So the paradox stands: men need to die if man is to survive. There is a profounder reality to death than that, however. Death has profound psychological importance. In the thought of Martin Heidegger death is the great key which qualifies man's whole existence. It stands at the boundary of his life and judges the use he makes of it. Man at birth is already dying, his very existence is a 'being towards death'.[4] Heidegger maintains that the fact that death is man's ultimate possibility means that it is the key category by which he must organise his life.

Heidegger's point is that death must be reckoned in with my possibilities. It need not be left as a loose end, an arbitrary and contingent happening that will one day befall me. It can be taken up into existence as the capital possibility before which all the others are stretched out and in the light of which they are to be evaluated.[5]

In other words, if there were no death at the end of the road for us, no terminus, no final moment, time would have no meaning and, as we are presently constituted, that would be disastrous. It would mean that we'd never achieve anything. Humans need the passing of time as a spur to achievement. Most of the great geniuses were men in a hurry, battling against the tyranny of time: Dickens, hacking away at the next instalment of one of his novels; Churchill battling urgently to achieve fame and success before launching himself into politics; our Lord himself, preaching constantly about the shortness of the time and the need for urgency, for the night was coming when no man could work. Once we have honestly and steadily accepted the certainty of our death, once we face up to its inevitability, our life should take on new meaning and purpose. Our life should be something achieved and not just something passed. Time should be filled with struggle and achievement and greatness because it is too short to waste on all those second-rate pursuits that devour our time and stunt the quality of our lives. There is so much to do, to see, to read, to walk on, to listen to, to pray for, to triumph over. The certainty of our death should give impetus to our life. I would like to think that one night all over the world millions of men will be sitting watching the same fourth-rate television show and into their minds at the same time will come a sense of the certainty of their death and the shortness of the time. And as one man they will stand up and switch the damned thing off. One by one the sets will go out all over the world. Then there will be a great surge of human achievement: libraries will be ransacked; churches will be prayed in; mountains will be climbed; music will be made; poetry will be read; history will be made and time will be devoured in achievement—all because 'from a proud tower in the town, Death lookes gigantically down'.[6]

Is that all? Is the only answer to the question of death a defiant courage? 'Man is perishable. That may be; but let us perish resisting, and, if it is nothingness that awaits us, then let us so live that it will be an unjust fate.'[7] Certainly, the passionate acceptance of our own death is preferable to the flight from death which characterises our culture, but it still leaves the fundamental problem unsolved. However we discipline ourselves to accept and even to use the certainty of death, it remains true that in death the glory and promise of man collapses in complete fiasco. We are forced to echo Tolstoy: 'nothing exists but death, and death should not be.' Is there an answer to the question of death?

I believe that an analysis of death leads us to a point where we must take a leap towards transcendence, as did our analysis of man's search for knowledge and security in an ultimately problematic universe.

Again, the evidence points beyond this life to a reality larger than the reality we experience. The contemplation of death can be the prelude to revelation.

A fascinating analysis of death is Ladislaus Boros' *The Mystery of Death*: 'Death is a man's first completely personal act, and is, therefore, by reason of its very being, the place above all others for the awakening of consciousness, for freedom, for the encounter with God, for the final decision about eternal destiny.'[8]

He supports his hypothesis by an analysis of what he calls 'the historical dialectic of existence'. By that he means that there are two curves of existence which run through the life of man and they do not finally cut till death. The first curve, which is visible and exterior, is the irreversible exhaustion of our vital reserves from fertilisation till death. At the same time there opens up the possibility of an inner ascent, an invisible and interior curve of existence. The more the outer man disintegrates the purer is seen to be the *possibility* of strengthening the inner emergence of spirit. By a subtle displacement of psychic energy, the gradual limiting and weakening of the outer man *can* lead to a corresponding strengthening and spiritu-alising of the inner man. Boros traces the process in several ways.

First of all, the curve of the outer man imposes a definite rhythm on our being. There are five major crises in life—birth, puberty, experience, climacteric, and dissolution—that confront the inner man with the need to make a decision. We are forced by life out of one situation into another and plans for a new state of being must be made. In each crisis can be discovered the primitive image of all emergencies—birth. The crisis of puberty leads to the experience of the absolute, an experience that enables a man to make the venture of establishing human contacts. He expresses the absolute in his mental makeup by youth's refusal to compromise and joyful acceptance of self-sacrifice.

> It is precisely from these absolutist attitudes that later a new crisis arises: the crisis of experience. In this a man attains an inner maturity, a manner of existence which may perhaps be less interesting and revolutionary, but which is on the other hand solid and firmly rooted in earthly reality.[9]

The crisis of experience leads to responsible citi-zenship. Then comes the crisis of climacteric when the middle-aged man faces the poverty of existence, a period characterised by discipline and self-denial and the loss of illusions. Finally, decline brings about dissolution, making possible the deepest spirituali-sation of life, the emergence of the wise old man, whose strength is spirit. Such men have transformed all the energy of life into person. The final crisis is death, when the two curves of existence coincide. With every diminution of his vital forces man kept discovering in himself a new potential for being more completely a person; an independent centre inside existence was coming into being. It would appear, therefore, that the personal element in its fullness can only emerge in death.

Secondly, man's experience of his external environment traces a similar curve. From childhood, man experiences in his life a gradual widening of the context in which he lives. He becomes gradually aware of his own power to transform things. Excitedly, he confronts a world which has yet to be created, marked by his power, made pliant to his will; but slowly he notices that his dream always exceeds his achievement. It is precisely where a man fully realises that he is not equal to the world and can no longer encompass it that it begins to grow into a metaphysical thing. A displacement, similar to the one we have already noticed, takes place. As the physical cosmos begins to shrink again there emerges a corresponding enlargement of the spiritual world. As the scope of his actual world shrinks, first of all to his home, then to his room and finally to the couch on which he lies, the old man holds a world of spirit in his trembling hands. If we follow the process to where the two curves intersect, we may get some idea of what happens in death.

Existential space in the physical sense shrinks until nothing is left, but at the same time the spiritually perceived world grows into the infinite. The boundaries of the spiritual world are pushed back and man stands before a perfected universe, now seen in its real, essential depth. This universe now becomes his final path; along this he has to make his courageous way to God, daring all in one last reckless step.[10]

My analysis may be unduly theoretical and speculative, but anyone who has ever known a saint whose existence seemed to verge on pure spirit, will have seen in life what I have tried to put in words. The highest reaches of human spirituality seem to confer an identity that is almost independent of the body and impervious to death. Boros has detected a dialectic in man's life as it moves towards death which demands a leap towards transcendence for its final resolution. Examining the problem of death pushes us to the brink of revelation or religious vision. As in our analysis of knowledge and man's experience of the transitoriness of life, we are brought to a frontier and two responses are possible.

The first response is to decide tragically that man's life is fundamentally absurd, that man is afflicted with a passion for meaning and purpose in a universe that is finally meaningless and without purpose. The signals of transcendence which man imagines he receives from a reality beyond himself are simply projections of his own longing onto the meaningless immensity that confronts him. At the end of all his longing stands the bleak and nullifying certainty of death. Man is alone in a vast and threatening universe and all his poetry and all his pain is meaningless. Sartre has summed it up: 'Man is a useless passion. To get drunk by yourself in a bar or to be a leader of the nations is equally pointless.'[11] A man can only respond defiantly with courageous despair, raised like a fist in the face of the great emptiness from which we come and towards which we go. In Hemingway's short story, 'A Clean Well Lighted Place', defiant sadness is put into the prayer of the waiter: 'Our nada which art in nada, nada be thy nada. Thy nada come . . . . 'Nada—nothing. We find the same bleak theme in the autobiography of Bertrand Russell. He says that he sought the ecstasy of sexual love throughout his life because it relieves 'that terrible loneliness in which one shivering consciousness looks over the rim of the world into the cold, unfathomable, lifeless abyss.'[12]

The other response is faith. Our analysis of man's search for knowledge indicated that his experience of the world forces him to ask questions which cannot be answered in the world's terms. He is forced to conclude either that life is fundamentally absurd or that it has a transcendent cause. The purpose of religious faith is to confirm in man the ineradicable conviction *which he already possesses* that his life has meaning. We have already noticed the paradox of Camus' commitment to a life of purposeful action in a fundamentally absurd world. We see the same paradox in Sartre and Russell, who have dedicated their lives to action of an almost religious intensity despite an overwhelming conviction of the final meaninglessness of life. Their lives seem to refute the philosophies on which they claim to base them. The man of religious faith, on the other hand, operates on the rational assumption that the convictions which most characterise him as a man point to the only cause which can sufficiently explain them, God. So he commits himself to the faith that the darkness which surrounds him and towards which he goes is a gracious darkness, alive with the being of God.

PART THREE

9

The Disclosure of God

IN PART TWO of this book I attempted to develop a rudimentary natural theology. Any such attempt assumes, as the description suggests, that man is by nature constituted to know God. Such knowledge is not something that comes entirely from outside; it is, in fact, the undergirding presupposition of all man's purposeful activity. For most men, however, the knowledge does not become reflective belief, belief at the bottom of the heart, not just at the top of the mind. Reflective and self-conscious belief, the bringing into the mind of what has hitherto been locked up in the heart, is usually the result of some concrete revelation. By some strange chemistry of faith our eyes are opened and we see him in whom we have all along believed. So vivid and compelling is the experience that men of faith describe it as a gift, never as a private achievement. Here, of course, we are on the threshold of mystery. Why do some men believe thus and not all men? Theologians have given many answers, none wholly successful. At their best the answers all underline the vicariousness of reflective belief: those who are called to believe stand somehow, as a sign and a witness to and on behalf of those who do not believe. The community of faith is a representative, priestly community called, by the strange mystery of divine election, to offer worship on behalf of the world. It follows that the fundamental task of any community of faith is the priestly task of worship. A Church, a community of those called to reflective and self-conscious belief, stands in history as a sign that in the end, God is the glory and destiny of man. Every other element in the Church's task derives from the primary element: mission, ethics, social and political involvement are all derivative and they become vacuous if they usurp the primary role of worship. In a ruggedly empirical culture that fact is the biggest cross the believer has to bear.

> If thou be the Son of God, command that these stones be made bread. (Matthew 4.3)

The believer has to reject the temptation to provide empirical verification for his faith. Like his Lord he has to reply, 'I have meat to eat that ye know not of.' (John 4.32). In a pragmatic, achievement-oriented culture the priestly vocation of worship sets up an agonising tension. In a later chapter we must discuss at greater length the 'style' of the priestly calling in the world.

I said above that reflective belief is usually 'the result of concrete revelation'. Theologians used to make a distinction between general and particular revelation. General revelation was that knowledge of God which was generally available to men by the use of their reason. Particular revelation came from concrete historical events which mediated quite specific experiences of God. Mascall puts the distinction very well. 'The God of natural theology, of whom we know only that he is the transcendent cause of the finite world and has whatever attributes necessarily follow from this, is at best a bleak and austere deity until natural theology is quickened and warmed by revelation.'[1]

Whether men actually *experience* a twofold revelation is arguable, but it is a useful theoretical device for the explication of faith. The Christian Church believes itself to be the guardian of a particular revelation. The record of that revelation has been handed down in the Church in what is called the New Testament—*New* because it claims to fulfil the historical longing of the Jewish Church as recorded in the *Old* Testament.

Before we can profitably begin to examine the New Testament we must have a perspective, a point from which we can evaluate and assess what we read. Mere reading would be a neutral exercise. If I may paraphrase the letter of James: 'The devils too can read, and tremble.' What I want to do before examining certain key aspects of the New Testament is to set forth a principle of interpretation. Remember the words of Jesus in the parable about the poor man Lazarus who lay at the gate of the rich man: 'They will pay no heed even if someone should rise from the dead.' 'They', of course, are the unbelievers. Though many men saw Jesus in the days of his flesh and witnessed his mighty acts, only a few had faith in him. I think, therefore, that we must note one absolutely fundamental thing. Christians believe that Christianity is a historical religion. By that we mean that God discloses his presence to us, not in timeless myths, but in actual, concrete historical events. Those events, however, are ambiguous. To the eyes of faith Jesus was the incarnation of God; but the same man provoked the response, 'Is not this Joseph's son?' Events can be taken at face value, or they can be seen in depth, by faith, as the revelation of God. It is crucial here to understand revelation and its mode of expression. The word simply means unveiling, opening up the real meaning of a thing, as when one is studying a code and suddenly everything fits into place, the light dawns, and the meaning is disclosed. St Paul says: 'All that may be known of God by men lies plain before their eyes.' (Romans 1.19). Very well so, but it also has to be said that it is not always as plain as Paul says it is. We have to have a key to open up the code of God's presence in the things that lie plain before our eyes. True, God comes to us in homely things like bread and wine or a Galilean carpenter, but his presence is hidden, veiled, until we see through the eyes of faith. Faith breaks the code. In the eucharistic hymn of Thomas Aquinas: 'Faith, our outward sense befriending, makes the inward vision clear.' I am not disputing the divine initiative in revelation, but the approach of God, the presence of God, requires the response of faith if we are to see all that may be known of God by men. The bare events are neutral, or it might be better to say are potential, until faith befriends the outward sense and we see things as they are beneath the outward sense.

> The essential condition of effectual revelation is the coincidence of divinely controlled event and minds divinely illumined to read it aright.[2]

I have laboured the point because understanding it is fundamental as we approach the New Testament. The New Testament is not a record of raw facts recorded and written down by neutral observers, like reporters at a football match. The publicly observable events of the career of Jesus of Nazareth do not come to us as in a newsreel, as raw facts, as events that lie plain before our eyes. They come to us already filtered through the faith of the early Church, already written down as seen in depth. Faith has already befriended the outward sense of the early Christians and we are seeing the object of their inward vision. Again, I do not mean to dispute the basic historicity of the events, but to recognise that we see them already interpreted by faith. They are already transposed into the language and categories of faith, the faith of the early Church.

We are presented already with the Christ of Christian faith.

> Something which has existed since the beginning,
> that we have heard,
> and we have seen with our own eyes;
> that we have watched
> and touched with our hands:
> the Word, who is life—
> this is our subject.
> That life was made visible;
> we saw it and we are giving our testimony,
> telling you of the eternal life
> which was with the Father and has been made
> visible to us.
> What we have seen and heard
> we are telling you
> so that you too may be in union with us,
> as we are in union
> with the Father
> and with his Son Jesus Christ.
> We are writing this to make our own joy complete.
>
> (1 John 1.1–4)

This, then, is our principle: *Historical facts, events, the things that can be clearly seen, are existentially neutral* —that is to say, they don't matter to us personally— until they are seen in depth. The New Testament is a record of certain historical events, but they are already in faith seen in depth and transposed into the language of faith. That is how we must see them if they are to become true for us. The point will become clearer if we look at certain key passages in the gospels.

This is how Jesus Christ came to be born. His mother Mary was betrothed to Joseph; but before they came to live together she was found to be with child through the Holy Spirit. Her husband Joseph, being a man of honour and wanting to spare her publicity, decided to divorce her informally. He had made up his mind to do this when the angel of the Lord appeared to him in a dream and said, 'Joseph son of David, do not be afraid to take Mary home as your wife, because she has conceived what is in her by the Holy Spirit. She will give birth to a son and you must name him Jesus, because he is the one who is to save his people from their sins.' Now all this took place to fulfil the words spoken by the Lord through the prophet:

The virgin will conceive and give birth to a son
and they will call him Emmanuel,

a name which means 'God-is-with-us'. When Joseph woke up he did what the angel of the Lord had told him to do: he took his wife to his home and, though he had not had intercourse with her, she gave birth to a son; and he named him Jesus. (Matthew 1.18–25)

In the sixth month the angel Gabriel was sent by God to a town in Galilee called Nazareth, to a virgin betrothed to a man named Joseph, of the House of David; and the virgin's name was Mary. He went in and said to her, 'Rejoice, so highly favoured! The Lord is with you.' She was deeply disturbed by these words and asked herself what this greeting could mean, but the angel said to her, 'Mary, do not be afraid; you have won God's favour. Listen! You are to conceive and bear a son, and you must name him Jesus. He will be great and will be called Son of the Most High. The Lord God will give him the throne of his ancestor David; he will rule over the House of Jacob for ever and his reign will have no end.' Mary said to the angel, 'But how can this come about, since I am a virgin?' 'The Holy Spirit will come upon you' the angel answered 'and the power of the Most High will cover you with its shadow. And so the child will be holy and will be called Son of God. Know this too: your kinswoman Elizabeth has, in her old age, herself conceived a son, and she whom people called barren is now in her sixth month, for nothing is impossible to God.' 'I am the handmaid of the Lord,' said Mary, 'let what you have said be done to me.' And the angel left her. (Luke 1.26–38)

People come to those texts with one of two attitudes. First, they may dismiss the whole matter as being, in principle, impossible. Things like that just don't happen in our orderly universe. It is a charming legend, an oriental fairy tale. More, it is a stumbling-block because it offends the commonsense of modern man, yet another of those needless offences which the Church insists on placing before men. The second attitude is equally uncompromising, although it does at least try to take the texts seriously. It tries to account for the story by imagining reasons for it:

1. It is told in order to square certain Old Testament prophecies.

2. Because Jesus made such a vivid impression on his disciples they read back glory into his birth.

3. The story rests on fact.

Let us consider those reasons:

1. The relevant verse here is Matthew 1.22: 'Now all this took place to fulfil the words spoken by the Lord through the prophet: The virgin will conceive and give birth to a son and they will call him Emmanuel.' Opponents of the Virgin Birth point out

that Matthew was not above doctoring a few facts to fit in some of his favourite Old Testament prophecies. That, they say, is obviously what he's done here. He found the prophecy and imagined a story to fulfil it. Here, actually, the reverse is true. The relevant quotation is Isaiah 7.14: 'Therefore the Lord himself shall give you a sign: behold a maiden shall conceive and bear a son and shall call his name Immanuel.' Far from doctoring the facts to suit the Old Testament, Matthew, is here doctoring the prophecies in the Old Testament to suit the facts! The Hebrew reads simply, 'young woman'. In the Greek version which Matthew probably used the word *can* mean virgin. So poor Matthew is really having to force a meaning on to prophecy which it almost certainly cannot bear. It cannot be said that the account of the Virgin Birth is an attempt to square with the Old Testament. This, in its way, would seem to move us some way towards accepting the narrative.

2. It can be said that it is certainly true that the total impression made by Jesus on the disciples is fundamental and that it colours their memory of him, but it is difficult to understand how the concept of a Virgin Birth should be suggested by their experience of Jesus, unless there were some factual evidence to commend it.

3. The evangelists state the Virgin Birth as a plain fact. They don't seem to be grinding any particular axe. No purpose would appear to be served by the

account other than stating that it happened. Thus it can be concluded, 'For history the really strong argument in favour of the Virgin Birth is the difficulty of accounting for the story otherwise than on the assumption of its truth.'[3]

We are left with the choice of rejecting the doctrine because of its *a priori* impossibility, or of accepting the doctrine because there seems to be no other credible way of explaining why it is given. Is that all that can be said? I think not. It seems to me that the story of the Virgin Birth has occasioned much needless controversy. I hope we can arrive at an understanding which is more satisfying yet less uncompromising than the two we've considered. Should anyone be scandalised by the doctrine he should not be deterred from Christian faith because of it. It has often been pointed out that the Virgin Birth is not explicitly mentioned by Paul, John, or Mark, although we can presume that each writer gives us an adequate account of the essentials of faith. We have to bear in mind in studying such passages what we considered above. The New Testament is the account given by the faith of the first Christians of the meaning and significance of Jesus. The real question to be asked is not, 'what is the level of factual truth in the event?' but, 'does the doctrine help us to explain or assess the significance of Jesus?' Does it enable us better to recognise God's presence in the birth and life of Jesus?

First, unlike the miracle of the resurrection, the Virgin Birth is not historically verifiable. It is a waste of time either to seek to defend or dispute its historicity. It may be that an attitude of what has been described as 'reverent agnosticism' is the safest approach to the historicity of the narratives, but to leave the matter suspended there is to miss the whole point. We must seek to discover the *theological* meaning of the narratives, and if we do so we strike gold. The story of the Virgin Birth coheres very well with our principle of interpretation, which is that Faith sees events in depth, detecting in them the initiative God, and responds in obedience. The double movement of divine initiative and human response constitutes what William Temple called 'effectual revelation'.

The two notes of divine initiative and human response are clearly detectable in the story of the Virgin Birth. The narratives set the origin of Jesus Christ in the context of a considered initiative of God. The birth of Christ was not the result of a human initiative, however splendid. It had its origin in 'the determinate counsel and foreknowledge of God' (Acts 2.23). It was a 'divinely controlled event'. The accounts of the Virgin Birth are thus important Christological documents which say that 'God was in Christ' from the beginning. They rule out an adoptionist or humanistic Christology. While God's revelation of himself in Christ was continuous with his revelation in the creation from the beginning (a theme which is examined in greater detail in the next chapter), in Jesus Christ there is a vast qualitative difference. In Christ a revelational leap occurs. There is a new creation, a new creative initiative on God's part, parallel only to his original initiative in creation. That is the primary note in the accounts of the Virgin Birth: the birth of Christ was a divinely controlled event.

The other note in the accounts is equally important. The event has its origin in God, but God's initiatives do not create an automatic response. God's initiatives, his reachings out toward us, demand for their effectiveness a free response from man. The prototype of faith is our Lady: 'Behold the handmaid of the Lord, be it done unto me according to thy word.' The glorious advent of God depends for its effectiveness on the obedience of a simple girl.

Far from being embarrassed by the accounts of the Virgin Birth in the gospels, I find them, in fact, very good introductions to the theological quality of the New Testament. We get into difficulties only if we ask the wrong questions and fail to recognise our overall principle—that in the New Testament faith speaks to faith of its Lord. 'Faith, our outward sense befriending, makes our inward vision clear.'

10

Who is Christ?

I TRIED to point out in the previous chapter that it is not very profitable either to take the New Testament literally or to leave it as childish make-believe. Neither attitude is really helpful in the long run. The New Testament is the account given by the faith of the early Church of Jesus Christ. Only when the objective events are seen in depth through faith do they confront us where we are, make our inward vision clear. While matters of fact and history do arise and are crucially important, the really primary matter is the 'theological' meaning of the New Testament. The question that we must bring to our study of the New Testament is, therefore, the one put by Professor Hodgson: 'What must the truth be, and have been, if it appeared like that to men who thought and wrote as they did?'

If we ask that question honestly we face a major dilemma. The language and thought forms of the writers of the New Testament are difficult for many people today. The impression given has been described with almost brutal frankness by the former Bishop of Woolwich in *Honest to God:* 'Jesus was really God

Almighty walking about on earth, dressed up as a man. Jesus was not a man born and bred . . . he was God for a limited period taking part in a charade. He looked like man, he talked like man, but underneath he was God dressed up—like Father Christmas . . . we are left with the impression that God took a spacetrip and arrived on this planet in the form of a man. Jesus was not really one of us; but through the miracle of the Virgin Birth he contrived to be born so as to appear one of us.'

This puts the spotlight on one of the most difficult New Testament categories for many to understand today: the pre-existence of Christ. There is no doubt that Christ's pre-existence is implicit in the gospels as well as explicit in the opening chapter of the letter to the Hebrews. What is the truth for us about Jesus Christ if the doctrine of his pre-existence was the best category which the New Testament writers could find to express the truth which they experienced? What is the truth about the pre-existence of Christ for us if we are unable to accept what Robinson calls the spaceship theory of the nature of Christ?

John MacQuarrie points out that the problem is not new. One hundred and fifty years after Christ, St Justin was asked by critics of Christianity whether the doctrine of the Incarnation meant that God had shown himself in the world only one hundred and fifty years before. St Justin answered that Christ is 'The Word of whom every race of men are partakers'. The Word was known among the Greeks who had lived according to it. It had spoken and acted in the Old Testament, for instance, in the burning bush. Finally, it had become flesh. St Justin was saying that while Jesus Christ is the revelation of God's presence and action in the world, he stands in continuity with God's action in the world *from the beginning*. The great events of the Old Testament as well as all genuine knowledge of God wherever it might be found are all of a piece with God's revelation in Christ. He finds it impossible to say that the truth of Christ appeared suddenly one hundred and fifty years earlier. All history has been showing the truth which we see with such glory in Christ. As Paul said, 'The things which may be known of God lie plain before our eyes.'

In other words, the doctrine of the pre-existence of Christ is a dramatic statement of the continuity of God's revelation of himself in history: 'When in former times God spoke to our forefathers, he spoke in fragmentary and varied fashion through the prophets. But in this the final age he has spoken to us in the Son' (Hebrews 1.1–2). It was the same God and the same Word of God working to disclose himself. I think that is fair both to the New Testament and to the truth, and yet it frees us from the embarrassment of trying to hold in our minds a concept uncongenial to us—the notion of a pre-existent being who swoops down into the body of a man. What of that body, however, what of

Jesus of Nazareth? If the doctrine of pre-existence safe-guards the great initiative of God in the Incarnation, what about the role of Jesus, true man?

It is here that we see the uniqueness of God's revel-ation in Christ. I said in Chapter 9 that there were two sides to effective revelation: The divine initiative (pre-served in the doctrine of pre-existence), and the human response. We saw that truth in the Virgin Birth: 'Be it unto me according to thy word.' In the language of the letter to the Hebrews every previous revelation of God had been 'fragmentary and varied', depending, as it did, on the fragmentary and varied responses of those through whom and to whom it was given. At last in Jesus of Nazareth came a man who lived the revelation with a complete and consuming totality of obedience, even unto death. So open to the initiative of God, he was a transparent vehicle of the Divine, so that Hebrews can say: 'He reflects the glory of God and bears the very stamp of his nature.' (Hebrews 1.3)

We can detect the dialectic between revelation and response if we examine another key passage in the New Testament—the account of the baptism and temptation of Jesus.

Then Jesus appeared: he came from Galilee to the Jordan to be baptised by John. John tried to dissuade him. 'It is I who need baptism from you' he said 'and yet you come to me!' But Jesus replied, 'Leave it like this for the time being;

it is fitting that we should in this way do all that righteousness demands.' At this, John gave in to him. As soon as Jesus was baptised he came up from the water, and suddenly the heavens opened and he saw the Spirit of God descending like a dove and coming down on him. And a voice spoke from heaven, 'This is my Son, the Beloved; my favour rests on him.' (Matthew 3.14–15)

The first thing to note about this story is that there can be little doubt that it happened. The fact that the early Church found it an embarrassment underlines its authenticity. John's baptism was 'a baptism of repentance for the forgiveness of sins'. It was very embarrassing for the disciples of a later time with their conviction of the sinlessness of Jesus. John the Baptist says to Jesus: 'It is I who need baptism from you and yet you come to me!' But Jesus replied, 'Leave it like this for the time being; it is fitting that we should, in this way, do all that righteousness demands.' Almost certainly, the story would not have been told unless it had happened and was well known. Still, we have to recognise that the fact of the baptism has been clothed in a greater significance by the faith of the Church and used to light up Jesus in depth as the Son of God. Jesus' baptism is narrated with a theological motive. What is that motive?

I said earlier that the action of God in the person of Jesus was continuous with his action in history: it is the same Word which is addressed to man. I also suggested that to be effective the revelation of God demands the response of man: the Word of God and the

Amen of man, true God and true man. The unique significance of Jesus is the totality of his response, the wholeheartedness of his Amen, his obedience even to death. In the baptismal narrative we see both poles: the action of God and the total commitment of Jesus. It is told as a story of vocation. At the decisive moment in his career Jesus responds to the call of God and commits himself fully to be the bearer of the Word. The price of his total commitment is already hinted at in the accounts, with their suggestion that Jesus understood his office as that of the Suffering Servant of Isaiah 42.1. 'Behold my servant, whom I uphold; mine elect, in whom my soul delighteth; I have put my spirit upon him.'

That understanding of the baptism seems to be underlined by the temptation stories which follow, of which there seems to be especially little point in asking about the historical 'fact' behind the narrative. The account is profoundly theological and supremely important for the argument of this book. The temptations are all temptations to surrender the uncompromising transcendentalism of the Gospel for the sake of a cheap and immediate acceptance by the world. The temptations all share a common emphasis: to limit the response of our Lord to his vocation by offering short cuts which will be less costly, less total in their demands upon him. The devil offers Jesus an immediate introduction to the cultured despiser of religion.

Then Jesus was led by the Spirit out into the wilderness to be tempted by the devil. He fasted for forty days and forty nights, after which he was very hungry, and the tempter came and said to him, 'If you are the Son of God, tell these stones to turn into loaves.' But he replied, 'Scripture says: Man does not live on bread alone, but on every word that comes from the mouth of God.'

The devil then took him to the holy city and made him stand on the parapet of the Temple. ' If you are the Son of God', he said, 'throw yourself down; for scripture says: He will put you in his angels' charge, and they will support you on their hands in case you hurt your foot against a stone.' Jesus said to him, 'Scripture also says: You must not put the Lord your God to the test.'

Next, taking him to a very high mountain, the devil showed him all the kingdoms of the world and their splendour. 'I will give you all these', he said, 'if you fall at my feet and worship me.' Then Jesus replied, 'Be off, Satan! For scripture says: You must worship the Lord your God, and serve him alone.'

Then the devil left him, and angels appeared and looked after him.

The first temptation, to make bread out of stones, suggests what is known as the social gospel. It is the temptation to good works, the temptation to reduce the Gospel to ethics. By ameliorating the material conditions of mankind we will justify ourselves in the eyes of the world. By letting our light shine before men they will see our good works and glorify us, follow us. Note the reply of Jesus: 'Man shall not live by bread alone.' He does not say that men don't need bread or houses or human rights or peace. He recognises implicitly the need for and the duty to supply such things—but not bread alone, because man's needs cannot be met on a purely material, ameliorative level. It is the temptation to foreshorten the wideness of the Gospel by foreshortening the needs of man: it is the temptation to turn the Gospel into sociology.

The second temptation is very like the first—to persuade people by wonders and gimmicks. Each is aimed at getting Jesus to take shallow, superficial and immediate action. Not only would that cheapen God, it would cheapen man too, and devalue his real needs. It makes the Gospel a cynical programme of bread and circuses for the blind and crude who have no needs beyond food and boredom. Jesus rejects that temptation, too, not only because he recognises the depth and grandeur of God, but also because he recognises the greatness of man. God's action in Christ would be at a level deeper than publicly observable marvels.

The third temptation to worship Satan is the temptation to worship the creation rather than the creator for the sake of success, a much more subtle temptation than the others. It is the temptation to accept man's assessment of his needs and man's means for meeting them. As a temptation it comes in many ways, not all of them crude. It is the Utopian temptation: the temptation to believe that, by manipulating man's environment and surroundings a society can be created that will increase his humanity. It is the temptation to make an exclusively political or sociological assessment of man. We note again a foreshortening of man's destiny, a curtailing of his significance. He becomes trapped in the things that merely appear.

Jesus rejects all the temptations. He refuses to limit his response, to cheapen or popularise his message by devaluing the profound destiny of man who can find his peace and glory only in doing God's will: 'You must worship the Lord your God, and serve him alone.'

11

Delivered Unto Glory

I SAID in the first part of this book that the Church is in permanent and unresolvable tension between preserving and celebrating the Gospel, and communicating that Gospel to the world. The tension is derived from the very life of our Lord. Jesus Christ is the fullest revelation of God which the world has known, and man and the world have felt the pressure of God's revealing of himself since history began. We can detect that pressure on our own lives in all those hints that point beyond themselves to a solution in a reality beyond the reality we experience in this world. Our experience of the world raises questions which the world cannot answer. There is a mysterious economy in God's relations with the world: he never overwhelms us; he requires our response; so God's revelation comes to man in 'diverse and fragmentary' ways, as diverse and fragmentary as the responses of man. God has never been without witnesses, but only in Jesus Christ has that witness been utterly transparent to the glory of God. He was a man total in his obedience, perfect in his response, the very incarnation of God. The agony and paradox of his response lies in the fact that Jesus did not cease to be a man. The glory of his nature lies in the fact that his life was an unremitting act of human obedience to the Father. His was an obedience that led, inevitably, to death. The agony of that vocation lay in the fact that Jesus, right up to the end, was tempted to dilute his perfect obedience to the Father for the sake of obedience to the insistent demands of the world. No gross temptation, it was temptation at its highest. It was the temptation to respond, in compassion, to the world's estimate of its own needs. There is plenty of evidence in the New Testament of the compassion of Jesus, the almost raging concern he had for the suffering of the world. Temptation came to him at the noblest level of his being. He was tempted to respond, in obedience, to the call of the world for bread and revolution. He was so tempted right to the night on which he was betrayed by Judas Iscariot, another key element in the New Testament account:

He was still speaking when Judas, one of the Twelve, appeared, and with him a large number of men armed with swords and clubs, sent by the chief priests and elders of the people. Now the traitor had arranged a sign with them. 'The one I kiss,' he said, 'he is the man. Take him in charge.' So he went straight up to Jesus and said, 'Greetings, Rabbi,' and kissed him. Jesus said to him, 'My friend, do what you are here for.' Then they came forward, seized Jesus and took him in charge. At that, one of the followers of Jesus grasped his sword and drew it; he struck out at the high priest's servant, and cut off his ear. Jesus then said, 'Put your sword back, for all who draw the sword will die by the sword. Or do you think that I cannot appeal to my Father, who would promptly send more than twelve legions of angels to my defence? But then, how would the scriptures be fulfilled that say this is the way it must be?' It was at this time that Jesus said to the crowds, 'Am I a brigand, that you had to set out to capture me with swords and clubs? I sat teaching in the Temple day after day and you never laid hands on me.' Now all this happened to fulfil the prophecies in scripture. Then all the disciples deserted him and ran away. (Matthew 26.47–56)

One of the cruellest riddles of history is why Judas betrayed Jesus. There are several possible reasons.[1]

1. An old tradition says that Judas was the nephew of Caiaphas the High Priest who was determined to get rid of Jesus. Judas was persuaded to become a secret undercover agent to plot the downfall of Jesus from within. Whether or not that theory is true, Judas certainly became a tool in the hands of the enemies of our Lord and he was used to bring about his arrest.

2. Another explanation is that Judas did it for the money. John tells us that Judas 'was a thief and had the bag and stole from it'. Judas seems to have been the treasurer of our Lord's band of disciples. If he was a thief as John maintains, writing a long time after, then it is just conceivable that Judas betrayed Jesus for the £5 reward that was offered.

Neither of these explanations produces a convincing reason for what Judas did. A better clue may lie in his name *Iscariot*. According to William Barclay, the word may be connected with the Latin word *sicarius*, a dagger-bearer, a knifer, a razor-man. The Sicarii were fanatical Jewish nationalists, professional revolutionaries who believed in the violent overthrow of their Roman masters. Judas may have belonged to that group. He may have seen in Jesus the heaven-sent leader, the great charismatic figure who could unite the country against the Roman occupation. When he realised that Jesus did not plan to take the way of armed revolt, he may have betrayed him into the hands of his enemies in sheer disgust. An embittered revolutionary might do that to someone whom he considered had deserted the cause. Even more likely, however, is the possibility that Judas was trying to force the hand of Jesus. By placing him in a position of danger, Judas thought, Jesus would react violently in his own defence and the revolution would be on. Judas was playing confrontation politics. He wanted the night of the long knives. Blood would flow. The Kingdom would be won by violence.

There are many indications in the gospel that Jesus loved Judas and had great hopes for him. The kiss need not have been hypocritical. Judas may have intended it as a signal of revolt. This is it, Master, the hour is here, buckle on your gunbelt and come. To his horror, Jesus allows himself to be taken. Such an explanation accounts well for what happened next.

> When he found that Jesus had been condemned, Judas his betrayer was filled with remorse and took the thirty silver pieces back to the chief priests and elders. 'I have sinned', he said. 'I have betrayed innocent blood.' 'What is that to us?' they replied, 'That is your concern.' And flinging down the silver pieces in the sanctuary he made off, and went and hanged himself. (Matthew 27.3–5)

Devastatingly Judas realises that he has delivered Jesus to death. In that moment he may also have realised the uselessness of the dream of revolt and political independence. In total despair he hangs himself. Whatever his motives, he enters history as the greatest traitor of them all: the man who delivered the Son of God to death.

The interpretation that sees Judas as a political revolutionary gives the story an incredibly modern ring. There's nothing like police action for activating your warm-hearted liberal! The radicalising of the reluctant leader is a common theme in our culture. One of the themes of the classic Western film is the good man, a deadly shot and a natural leader of men, who returns to a small town and hangs up his gun. One day the town is invaded by desperate characters who terrorise the local populace. At first the good man does nothing; he has renounced violence and hung up his gun. Then comes the moment every boy loves: the great catharsis. With nerve-straining deliberateness, the hero fastens on his gunbelt and strides out into the dusty main street to take on the bandits single-handed.

Was Judas trying to force Jesus into a 'high noon' situation like this? If so, Jesus refused to take the bait. He went, instead, to the cross.

Why?

What was the message of Jesus? He came using certain words, words with commonly accepted meanings, but he used them in an unusual way. A common and sentimental fallacy is abroad about Jesus. People say that his message was simple and understandable, unlike the complicated prolixities of modern theologians. In fact, the simple Jesus is very difficult to discover in the New Testament. His teaching was a source of puzzled speculation to those who heard him, even among his disciples. Mark even suggests that Jesus deliberately made his teaching enigmatic so that those 'outside . . . may see and see again, but not perceive; may hear and hear again, but not understand; otherwise they might be converted and be forgiven.' (Mark 4.12). The central core of his teaching was, to the end, profoundly ambiguous. Jesus came announcing a Kingdom.

After John had been arrested, Jesus went into Galilee. There he proclaimed the Good News From God. 'The time has come,' he said, 'and the kingdom of God is close at hand. Repent, and believe the Good News.' (Mark 1.14–15)

It is hard to blame his fellow Jews for failing to understand him. The Jews were a proud people, but they were a subject race, a race which had been led into slavery time and again. They longed for liberation, for self-government, for the kingdom to be restored to Israel. Like the old Jacobites of Scotland, they longed for their king to return. Then came Jesus announcing the nearness of the kingdom of God. Like most of us, instead of listening to him and trying to understand what he said, his hearers poured onto him all their hopes. They assumed that he had come to fulfil them in the way they wanted. 'Command these stones to become bread.'

We can understand if we put ourselves in their place. If a prophet came to Scotland in 1972 with the message, 'Independence is at hand. Repent, and believe in the Good News', what would be the general response? Many people in Scotland long for Scotland to be an independent nation. They have a great deal of general support but no real leader has caught the public imagination. If one came preaching a Gospel of Independence, few would ask 'independence from what?' They would assume that it was their sort of independence he was talking about, and they'd try to make him their leader just as the Jews tried to make Christ a king.

Well, what did Jesus mean by using those words? What was Jesus up to and why were people confused by his message? Before attempting to answer the most fundamental question that can be asked of Christian faith, I want to avoid a fundamental misconception.

While Christ refused to offer political leadership and said that man's real needs were deeper than political solutions could reach, he also directed his disciples to engage in politics, to involve themselves in society; and he was deeply engaged, on one level, himself. Let me explain.

William Temple was fond of saying that Christianity is the most materialistic of all religions. He meant that God had chosen matter to communicate himself to men. The Christian faith is a sacramental faith. It believes that God comes to man through the very stuff of creation. God has loaded this world with his glory; it is ablaze with the terrible beauty of God. In Matthew's chapter 25, we discover the absolutely frightening equation: to minister to the hungry and the homeless, the poor and the prisoner is to minister to Christ himself! Christ is the very stuff and motive of politics! God has so constituted his universe that everything is terrifyingly holy. To refuse to struggle for a better society and a more just world is to turn your back on God, because God has chosen to reveal himself not only in bread and wine and word, but in slum and trench and brothel. God has so constituted his universe that if we would engage ourselves with him then we must also engage ourselves with our neighbour. Ours is a starkly incarnational religion. God comes to us not only in the peace and reassurance of worship and prayer, but also in the unavoidable realities of flesh and blood. He comes to us in Everyman. He is the man who lives out his life in every evil and substandard house. He is the man who is blown apart in every air-raid. He is every shuffling derelict who fights for a bottle. If we open our eyes we'll find him strung up on a cross on numerous corners in numberless cities, crying for a love that we are supposed to bear. None of us can escape him, for he said: 'Inasmuch as you did it not to one of the least of these, you did it not to me.'

If, then, Christ commanded us thus to serve our neighbour, why did he not try to organise politically to fight for reforms or freedom? Why didn't he join Judas? Because politics tells only part of the truth about man and it can fulfil only part of his need. We must have the bread that politics provides. We must have houses and food and clothes, and such things must be fairly shared; but man does not live by those things alone nor does he find happiness when those things are multiplied. The truth is that man is a spiritual being and his real needs, his most characteristic needs, are deeper than the satisfactions of the body. Man's tragedy is that he was made for God and has wandered far from him. The kingdom he really longs for is the Kingdom of God, the fellowship of the Father, but he has forgotten or refuses to acknowledge it. So he wanders through history, seeking rest and finding none. He is filled with a terrible thirst for the living God but, like a traveller in the desert who mistakes a mirage for an oasis, he is constantly chasing substitutes for God. History is strewn with the wreckage of shattered utopias and abandoned dreams. 'Once I built a castle. Now it's down. Buddy, can you spare a dime?'

Christ knew all about it. He knew that only God was big enough to fill the aching gap in man's being. He was tempted to give men the substitutes they wanted: the kingdoms of this world and their glory; bread and circuses; revolutions and the terrible going forth of armies; but he knew that those things were not the answer to the deepest needs of man. Instead he announced that by fellowship with him men could find fellowship with God; and he said that fellowship with God was the only thing man essentially required because it was the only thing that time and death could not take away. Thieves could not break through and steal it. Rust and moth could not corrupt it. When all else failed it would endure. All man's proud castles would fall. Sand would cover his civilizations. Death would strip the flesh from his bones. Nothing could touch his fellowship with God. That would endure.

That was the message of Christ. It is just as electrifyingly relevant as it was two thousand years ago. If Jesus had been the kind of revolutionary leader that Judas wanted him to be, or if he'd been simply the kind of social reformer people make him out to be, he would not be remembered, let alone worshipped, today. History would have obliterated his message because it would not have been relevant outside the social and political context of first-century Palestine. Man's social and political environment changes with every generation, but one thing does not change: all men, everywhere and at all times, are searching whether they know it or not for fellowship with God, because that is what they were made for. Jesus came to announce that he was the way to that fellowship with God. In him, the Kingdom of God was in their midst. The Christian Church stands today in witness to that final reality which has been set up for all men to see.

There are no new problems in theology, only the old ones in modern dress. It is sad to see theologians today so busily falling for the hoary temptations of old. With the best intentions, many theologians today are reinterpreting the Christian gospel along lines specifically rejected by our Lord. They exhort the Church to deliver the bread, to act consciously as an organised agent for social change, to align herself with the wave of revolutionary unrest which is sweeping the world. In truth, however, the task of the Church in the world today is much more agonising than that, because it is much more dialectical. Christians are indeed to engage in re-shaping the world, but with certain characteristic qualifications. In the first place, they will do it with a certain realism because they know that there is no fundamental security in this world and no final kingdom can be fashioned from it. That realism should free the Christian from the totalitarian spirit which makes revolutions possible and corrupts them as they are made. The Christian above all men should be aware of the transience and vulnerability of man. There is something of such wistful awareness in Paul's exhortation to the Corinthians: 'Those who have to deal with the world should not become engrossed in it. I say this because the world as we know it is passing away.' (1 Corinthians 7.31)

The second qualification flows from that. The Christian should engage in the world with a leaven of pity. *Pity* may be a timid word to use, but it seems to me to be the right one. In *Darkness at Noon*, an account of the horrors of revolutionary Russia, Arthur Koestler begins with these words from Dostoevsky: 'Man, man, one cannot live quite without pity.' That seems to me to be an essential ingredient in all man's political activity if it is to remain human, and it should be the mark of the Christian's engagement in politics. Pity is an unspectacular virtue, compounded of humour and a rueful awareness that you're really no better than those with whom you disagree. There is something of it in Auden's 'Let us love one another before we die'. It is bred of a loving awareness of the vulnerability of all men. Pity blunts the edge of revolutionary ardour because it suddenly gives glimpses of the wistfulness of the people who are supposed to be hated. It disarms you in the face of the virulent racist who weeps over the loss of his child. It overwhelms you in the face of the rich man whose wife has left him with nothing except his wealth. Somehow, we are all out in the cold. For the Christian, the sense of the pathos of man should be overpowering. It was the mark of Christ.

> O Jerusalem, Jerusalem, which killest the prophets and stonest them that are sent unto thee; how often would I have gathered thy children together as a hen doth gather her brood under wings, and ye would not! (Luke 13.34)

In an age in which politics is increasingly characterised by hatred and a carefully articulated intolerance, the Christian can participate only in the spirit of pity.

The Christian must finally realise that the task of the Church is not fundamentally ethical or political. It is not even fundamentally evangelistic, though, as we have seen, it is under permanent orders to evangelize. The Church's primary task is to witness to the reality for which Christ gave himself to death: the Kingdom of God. The Church stands in history as a sign to man that although this world passes it does not have the final word, because God's day will come and, in Christ, we have already received an assurance of its triumph. Man's tragedy is not final. Beyond that tragedy God has prepared a better thing for him: a kingdom, eternal in the heavens.

> Pilate said unto him . . . Art thou the King of the Jews? Jesus answered, My kingdom is not of this world: if my kingdom were of this world, then would my servants fight, that I should not be delivered to the Jews: *but now is my kingdom not from hence.* (John 18.33 ff.)

12

Resurrection

IS THAT all? Are we left then with the memory of yet another tragic hero, winsome but powerless on a cross? That is not the witness of the New Testament. The books of the New Testament were written in the certain conviction that Jesus Christ was raised from the dead 'on the third day'.

> And now, my brothers, I must remind you of the gospel that I preached to you; the gospel which you received, on which you have taken your stand, and which is now bringing you salvation. Do you still hold fast the Gospel as I preached it to you? If not, your conversion was in vain.
>
> First and foremost, I handed on to you the facts which had been imparted to me: that Christ died for our sins, in accordance with the scriptures; that he was buried; that he was raised to life on the third day, according to the scriptures; and that he appeared to Cephas, and afterwards to the Twelve. Then he appeared to over five hundred of our brothers at once, most of whom are still alive, though some have died. Then he appeared to James, and afterwards to all the apostles.
>
> In the end he appeared even to me.(1 Corinthians 15.1–8)

We must be quite certain of the claim being made here. It is difficult, because centuries of popular preaching have overlaid the staggering events with a veneer of embarrassed sentiment. Most preachers and many theologians are significantly silent about what happened in that hour between night and day in the garden where they laid him. After all, how does an educated twentieth-century man deal with a miracle? One thing he does is to poetise it. The fact that Easter comes in the spring in our hemisphere is a godsend to the preacher. He talks about the death of winter and the rebirth of spring. He talks about bulbs sprouting and lambs leaping, about the birth of hope after the death of despair. He will talk about any or all of those things and suggest that they are the miracles the resurrection is all about. He'll imply that the body of Jesus, like John Brown's, may lie mouldering in the grave but his beautiful soul goes marching on. He'll suggest that the fragrance of that holy life lingers on. He'll claim that the example of Jesus so infected his followers that he lives on in their lives. All these things, he'll claim, are what the resurrection is about.

Of course, they're not. Matthew tells us that the Jews sealed the tomb with a stone and set a watch upon it, just in case his followers came to steal the body. Many modern preachers make the tomb just as secure by smothering it in rhetoric and embarrassed sentimentality. The New Testament does nothing of the sort. It says simply that he rose from the dead and was seen by the brethren. It doesn't say how it happened, but it says with defiant certainty *that* it happened. It was that certainty which sent the apostles out into the world, no longer fearful, but with a heady nonchalance which faced death and suffering gladly and changed the course of history. Probably the most imposing evidence for the resurrection is that courageous ease of the apostles. What else could have transformed a dispirited bunch of deserters into a community which turned the world upside down?

Mostly the resurrection is dismissed on the basis of sweeping *a priori* assumptions. MacQuarrie takes issue with all such objections in his discussion on Bultmann's attitude to the resurrection.

Can we have any objective-historical understanding of the Resurrection? Bultmann thinks not. 'Is it not a completely mythical event?' he asks. And here we must take Bultmann to task for what appears to be an entirely arbitrary dismissal of the possibility of understanding the resurrection as an objective-historical event. He dismisses it because of some prior assumption in his mind. What is that assumption? . . . It is the hang-over of liberal modernism. . . . The resurrection, however we might understand it, would be miraculous in character, and Bultmann has decided in advance that in this scientific age we cannot believe in miracles, and therefore we cannot believe in the resurrection as an objective event that once happened, even if we can believe in it in some other way.

The fallacy of such reasoning is obvious. The one valid way in which we can ascertain whether a certain event took place or not is not by bringing in some sweeping assumption to show that it could not have taken place, but to consider the historical evidence available, and decide on that. But Bultmann does not take the trouble to examine what evidence could be adduced to show that the resurrection was an objective-historical event. *He assumes that it is myth.*[1]

Why do perfectly good Christian theologians like Bultmann simply dismiss the possibility of a miraculous resurrection? The answer is simple. What MacQuarrie calls 'the hangover from liberal-modernism' is the conscious or unconscious absorption by Christians of the dominant assumptions of the age. Where such assumptions are contrary to the beliefs of the Church the theologian has to develop elaborate rationalisations to justify his faith. His vocabulary is that of faith but most of his assumptions belong to the culture he inhabits.

One of the unquestioned assumptions of our age is that the universe works like a vast, preprogrammed machine. It is like an enormous clock which was wound up at the beginning of creation and goes ticking away, according to a more or less predetermined plan. There is no room for miracles in a clockwork universe. Everything happens because something else happened, which happened because something else happened. There are no interventions from beyond. There are two versions of the theory. The atheist believes that the universe wound itself up, so to speak, back in the mists of time. The theist believes that God wound it up. They both agree that however it got wound up, the thing is on its own now and no intervention is allowed. Since their theory prohibits any direct intervention of God in the resurrection or elsewhere, we are reduced to elaborate explanations within strictly defined categories. The resurrection becomes a subjective psychological experience of the disciples at the highest, or my personal, existential response to Jesus Christ at the lowest. Either way, the real action in the resurrection is human. No intervention of divine power is allowed. The bones of Jesus still lie on some Galilean hillside. What counts is how *you* respond to his memory.

Whatever else it may be that is not what the New Testament says. Paul is quite clear.

> Now if this is what we proclaim, that Christ was raised from the dead, how can some of you say there is no resurrection of the dead? If there be no resurrection, then Christ was not raised; and if Christ was not raised, then our gospel is null and void, and so is your faith; and we turn out to be lying witnesses for God, because we bore witness that he raised Christ to life, whereas, if the dead are not raised, he did not raise him. (1 Corinthians 15.12–15)

Rather than temporise with our explanations, would it not be more honest to confess, once and for all, that we have 'gone native' and, with the spirit of the age, rejected the Resurrection?

The New Testament is quite clear about the resurrection. The resurrection is a divine event. Jesus did not rise from the dead, he was raised, and there is a world of difference in the moods. We are dealing with a new creative act of God and to grapple with its meaning we must push all human categories from our minds. The only possible parallel we can find to the resurrection is the creation itself. According to Christian theology the creation was an act of God *ex nihilo*, and the only way to prepare ourselves for the majesty of the resurrection is to immerse ourselves in wonder at the creation. Steady contemplation of the creation should dispose us to that wonder which is the prelude to revelation. We obviously cannot waste time debating whether creation was an event in time and therefore historical. It is the *fact* of creation which is miraculous: why there is something at all and not just nothing. Creation itself is the great *a priori* assumption which shatters all shallow mechanistic categories of causation. Creation is a divine act. It is a supreme act of grace. God said 'Let there be', and there was! Only that can prepare us for the resurrection, for there is a new act of creation, a new 'let there be'. The resurrection shatters all human categories as it explodes all human power. 'For Christ was crucified through weakness yet he liveth through the power of God.' By creation God constituted matter and by resurrection he has raised it to an imperishable glory. At this point the 'cultured despiser' swallows hard and smiles. He knows (does he not) that matter, bone and gristle and hair, decay and turn to dust, yet the Christian insists on a double wonder. We are dust and to dust we shall return—but, as Augustine said, 'Out of the dust God has already made man; and to dust he gave life.' He has already performed one immense act of grace in the creation—he has given life to dust! More, much more, even than that: in Christ, Augustine goes on, 'he hath brought this dust to the Kingdom of Heaven'! In Christ God is performing another act of unimaginable grace which we can understand only as a new creation. Dust we were. Yes. He made us man, from that dust. To dust we return again. Yes. All men go down into the grave and become dust, but the resurrection of Christ proclaims a great new fact: one man has been raised from dust to imperishable glory. One man's bone and gristle and hair has been reconstituted to an unbearable weight of glory! We mustn't shrink from the words. We are talking about a fact, an event besides which all history pales into anticlimax. We are talking about a fact or we are talking about the biggest hoax in history. Paul understood it very clearly. Either Christ was risen or the Church has committed a massive perjury, 'because we swore in evidence before God that he had raised Christ to life'. If Christ was not raised, Paul goes on, 'Why are we living under a constant threat? I face death every day, brothers, and I can swear it by the pride that I take in you in Christ Jesus our Lord.' Do men go joyfully to death in the name of a lie they have perpetrated? If we can only shake ourselves free from the puny wisdom of our age and accept the apostolic witness to the mighty act of God we might recapture some of their revolutionary *élan*!

Can we ask what really happened in that tomb? Yes, but only poetry can hint at an answer. We know

125

the resurrection only through its effects, just as we can know the creative word of God only through its results in the natural creation. There are hints, though only a poet would grasp them.

I do not think that I would have looked straight at the tomb if I had been there, at the large boulder that they had rolled up to seal it with. I do not think that I could have even if I had wanted to, in that queer seething light between night and daybreak when you cannot look long at anything before it begins to disappear. I would have looked just above it, or off to one side.

One of the guardsmen asleep on the ground, his helmet resting in the crook of one arm, his other arm flung out on the damp grass. He stirs in his sleep and murmurs something unintelligible. Then, lying there on his back in the dark, he suddenly opens his eyes: the fire of a billion stars.

Or the leaves of an olive tree, gray green, unmoving in the still air. Nothing moves. Then, out of nowhere, a breeze comes up—stiff and fresh and smelling of the dawn: underneath, each olive leaf is the colour of silver.

A voice is shouting, high and soft and from far away like the voice a child hears calling him home, at the end of a long summer dusk. The sound of running feet.

I cannot tell you anything more than this about what I think I would have seen if I had been there myself. No man can honestly. I do not believe that even the ones who actually were there could have told you more, if any were there and stayed awake.

But I can tell you this: that what I believe happened and what in faith and with great joy I proclaim to you here is that he somehow *got up*, with life in him again, and the glory upon him. And I speak very plainly here, very unfancifully, even though I do not understand well my own language. I was not there to see it any more than I was awake to see the sun rise this morning, but I affirm it as surely as I do that by God's grace the sun did rise this morning because that is why the world is flooded with light.[2]

We cannot tell how it was that morning but with Paul we proclaim: 'But Christ has in fact been raised from the dead, the first-fruits of all who have fallen asleep.'

What, then, is the significance of the mighty act, the raising of Jesus Christ from the dead? Well, first of all, the resurrection has immense cosmic significance. Paul uses two words in describing the resurrection; he calls it both *aparxe* and *arrabon*. The word *aparxe* is usually translated *first-fruits* and it refers to the first harvest sheaf reaped, which was offered as a gift of God. The first sheaf is a pledge and promise as well as a beginning of the harvest. The resurrection of Christ, says Paul, is the first sheaf in the whole harvest of creation. The reconstitution and glorification of the man Jesus Christ is a pledge and promise of the reconstitution and glorification of all things.

> As he is the Beginning,
> he was first to be born from the dead,
> so that he should be first in every way;
> because God wanted all perfection
> to be found in him
> and all things to be reconciled through him and for him,
> everything in heaven and everything on earth,
> when he made peace
> by his death on the cross. (Colossians 1.18–20)

The exact force of *aparxe* can be underlined by considering another characteristic Pauline word, which, in places, seems to be virtually interchangeable with it: *arrabon*.

> From the beginning till now the entire creation, as we know, has been groaning in one great act of giving birth; and not only creation, but all of us who possess the first-fruits of the Spirit (*ten aparxen tou pneumatos*), we too groan inwardly as we wait for our bodies to be set free. (Romans 8.22–23)
> Yes, we groan and find it a burden being still in this tent, not that we want to strip it off, but to put the second garment over it and to have what must die taken up into life. This is the purpose for which God made us, and he has given us the pledge of the Spirit (*ton arrabona tou pneumatos*). (2 Corinthians 5.4–5)

Arrabon is a commercial term which signifies a pledge which is later returned; a deposit which pays part of the total debt and gives a legal claim, earnest money, ratifying a compact.

> And he said, I will send thee a kid from the flock. And she said, Wilt thou give me a pledge (*arrabon*) till thou send it? And he said What pledge shall I give thee? And she said, thy signet, and thy bracelets, and thy staff that is in thine hand. (Genesis 38.17 f.)

Both *aparxe* and *arrabon*, therefore, have an ineradicable future reference. They always imply acts which engage to something bigger; they start a process which runs on to a larger completion. They are terms of hope, pledges for the future. Paul trumpets the amazing message that in the resurrection of Jesus Christ God has given us a pledge and promise of the redemption of the whole of creation from change and decay. God has given us a blazing foretaste of his plan for the whole creation.

> He has let us know the mystery of his purpose, the hidden plan he so kindly made in Christ from the beginning, to act upon when the times had run their course to the end: that he would bring everything together under Christ, as head, everything in the heavens and everything on earth. (Ephesians 1.9–10)

The process has been set in motion in Christ! Even now the whole creation is being transformed! It is no wonder the apostles and first Christians went out and transformed the world, for they knew what creation was up to; God had let them know, by the raising of Christ from the dead, the mystery of his purpose for the whole created order. With such a massive understanding what could prevail against them? Only when the Church returns to a total conviction of the reality and power of the resurrection will she be re-endowed with the revolutionary *élan* of the apostles. The Church either witnesses to the resurrection or she is nothing!

The resurrection also has immense personal significance. One of the dominant tendencies in recent theology, as this book has tried to show, has been to reduce or foreshorten the Gospel: it becomes a guide or a programme for man's life on earth, but it is silent on the subject of his death. At its best, it steels us to sombre courage in the face of the great emptiness to which we go. It foreshortens hope to this life, this world, by offering dreams for some sort of collective future, but it has no word to me at the certain knowledge of my own death. Dust I am and unto dust I shall return. That is my agony. I am dust, yet I rebel against the fact. I rail against the certainty of my own extinction. 'Wretched man that I am, who will deliver me from the body of this death?'

The Christian answer to that cry is a very old though newly fashionable little word: *hope*. Hope, *elpis*, is another key word in Paul's understanding of the resurrection. In the Old Testament *elpis* does not project its own view of the future: it consists rather in general confidence in God's protection and help. *God* is the hope or confidence of the righteous. In the Greek notion of *elpis*, hope is that foresight which works with controllable factors. To Old Testament man, hope is directed to him who cannot be controlled. Everything in the earthly present is provisional and hope becomes increasingly hope in the eschatological future.

The New Testament depends on the Old Testament in its use of *elpis*. Hope is fixed on God. It has three elements: (1) expectation for the future; (2) trust; (3) the patience of waiting. Hope trusts to the degree it cannot count on controllable factors. *Elpis* cannot relate to 'the things that are seen' because everything visible belongs to the world on which no hope can be founded. Christian hope rests on the divine act of salvation accomplished in Christ, so hope is an eschato-logical blessing, a promise already fulfilled. It is im-portant to understand the utterly radical nature of Christian hope. It is not just a confident expectation of the future, though it is certainly that. Paul suggests in 1 Corinthians 13 that even when the consummation has been achieved, when we will know God as fully as we are known by him, *hope will endure*. That is because hope is not concerned with the realisation of a human dream in the future but with the confidence which waits for God's gift and, when it is received, does not rest in possession but in the assurance that God will maintain what he has given. Even in the consummation, Christian existence is inconceivable without hope. The radical conception of *elpis* removes the ground from any security in man as himself. We are destined, as men, to return to dust. Only God can raise that dust to newness of life. Only God supports man in his overwhelming contingency, and even in the consummation at the resurrection of the dead, man's new life will remain an eternal gift of God in Christ. In other words, Christian hope is that abiding trust in God who called us out of nothing and sustains and will sustain us in life. We have no security in our-selves, no false hopes, no naïve longings. Our only ground of hope is the God who raised Jesus Christ from the dead as 'the first-fruits of them that slept'. Paul's teaching on *elpis* is one with his conception of the radical nature of Grace. In man's dealings with

God everything is Grace, everything is gift. Our expectation for the future is rooted in a patient and profoundly trustful waiting on God alone. Our expectation does not reside in our own undying essence—or even in our own dying essence—or that we have been delivered from death and sin into an already-realised resurrection life. Rather, our expectation lies in the promises of a reliable God who has already, in Christ, set the action of our resurrection in motion. Christ's resurrection is the assurance and the beginning of our resurrection—it is both *arrabon* and *aparxe*, a pledge and a beginning.

We are indeed dust and to dust we shall return; but as Augustine has told us,

> We have begun to be some great thing. Let no man despise himself. We were once nothing, but we are something. . . . We had said, 'Remember that we are dust'; but out of the dust he made man, and to dust he gave life, and in Christ he hath brought this dust to the kingdom of heaven, he who made heaven and earth.[3]

We deduce two important consequences from that. First, in the face of death Christians do have a confident hope in the reliability of God who will, by an act of creative grace as certain as it is mysterious, raise them to newness of life. Second, a thoroughly humanised or secularised interpretation of Christian hope is, in Paul's words, a 'wretched doctrine'. It is wretched for two related reasons: (1) It is unable to sustain hope beyond the mournful finality of death; and (2) as a consequence it 'humanises' hope into a utopian wish for the future of man's world, based on history and ethics. The naïveté of such a view is unable to sustain man in the face of the ineradicable tragedy of existence. Only God can deliver us from tragedy. That, according to Paul, is precisely the Gospel: against all reductionist eschatology he trumpets the radical confidence of Christian hope. Death will be conquered and God will be in total and direct control of all things. The battle has begun and the outcome is not in doubt. Meanwhile, we must live in the time before the end. Meanwhile we must live in the joyful patience of Hope, for death has been robbed of its sting.

> Death be not proud, though some have called thee
> Mighty and dreadfull, for, thou art not soe,
> For, those, whom thou think'st, thou dost overthrow,
> Die not, poore death, nor yet canst thou kill mee.
>   why swell'st thou then?
> One short sleepe past, wee wake eternally,
> And death shall be no more; death, thou shalt die.
>   —John Donne

13

The Church

IN PART TWO of this book I attempted to show that there is a grace in creation which enables men to come to a genuine, if limited, knowledge of and relationship with God. God is present to men all through their lives as creator and sustainer. His presence is an insistent pressure on their lives, leading them to recognise him in those moments of disclosure which all men face. Life and creation are sacramental; they are vehicles of God's grace and presence. The sacramental way of encountering God respects man's terrible freedom to reject God, because a sacrament is, by definition, non-coercive. A sacrament demands a free, inter-pretative response from man; in it, God does not force himself upon man. With great tenderness and reticence *he suggests* his presence to man by the symbols of creation and life. He is present to man in all his decisions, in all his acceptance of the responsibility of moral choice, in all his longing for stability and peace, as well as in the thrill of search and adventure. I suggested three ways in particular in which hints of transcendence may appear to the man, alert to them.

First, in his attempt to understand and interpret his life in the world, man comes to a number of boundaries or, in Ogden's phrase a series of 'limiting questions'. At those frontiers of understanding man is faced with the knowledge that the world and his life in the world cannot be explained in terms of itself. He reaches a point of knowing 'that empirical knowledge is not adequate to the reality' which he is. He reaches the frontier of mystery, but because he is man he is an incorrigible searcher for answers. He must render such reason of the mystery as he is able to, and so he finds within himself an assurance, a confidence in the meaning of life which points to a transcendent reality beyond life which gives meaning and purpose to it. He is brought to the frontier of revelation.

Furthermore, man discovers in his journey through life that he is never entirely at home *in* life. Life brings him a strange passion for fulfilment accompanied by a mysterious sense of loss. He is afflicted with a desire which no natural happiness seems able to satisfy. Again he is brought to a strange frontier of desire. He is afflicted with a longing that wanders, uncertain of its object, seeking rest and finding none. Once more he is brought to the borderline of mystery, the frontier of revelation, because only in the unchanging reality of God is his longing for stability satisfied.

Finally, in his experience of death man is brought to the last frontier of all. Death affronts man. It seems to him not an inevitable biological fact, but an obscenity that reduces his deepest experiences to absurdity.

> Because of this absurdity there has risen through the ages a whole literature of protest against death, which is either presented as a constructional error in the work of creation, or else as the end of everything—which again is contradicted by all sorts of irrepressibly strong suggestions pointing towards a person's continued existence after death by the continued life of the soul.[1]

Man's experience of death nudges him again towards the edge of mystery, the frontier of revelation.

Other 'rumours of transcendence' in man's experience could be multiplied but they all leave man strangely unsatisfied. In Mascall's words, they lead us at best to 'a bleak and austere deity until natural theology is quickened and warmed by revelation'. We can accept his words, but we must recognise that God's grace is in his creation even where it is not 'warmed' by the historical revelation in Christ. We must also recognise that hints of transcendence are genuine revelations. They are not simply a human construct, a beggarly natural religion; they are active proof of God's gracious initiative in his dealings with man. Even where the historical revelation in Christ is not known, God is not without witnesses. All men are included in God's general will for salvation, with grace already living and working in their hearts. Even so, God has prepared a better thing for all men by his revelation of himself in his Son Jesus Christ our Lord, and that revelation in Christ is of a piece with his revealing of himself from the beginning. This is the real meaning of the Church's claim that Christ existed with the Father before all ages. The Word who became flesh was the Word of God who has informed all man's religious striving from the beginning. There is a continuity between the Christian revelation and all genuine religious knowledge.

Even in the historical revelation in Christ, however, God's self-disclosure respected man's freedom. His being among men was still sacramental. He did not coerce. His presence was veiled until men had eyes to see. The New Testament scriptures are the testimony of those whose eyes were opened to the revelation of God in Christ. Their testimony does not coerce man, but with the faith man can discern the revelation.

In chapter 11 I suggested that, in keeping with his manner of dealing with his creation, God's revelation demands for completeness the total response of man; but only in Jesus Christ has that response been complete. Only in him do we see the full glory of God; Christ's obedience was so total that he was utterly transparent to the glory of God. We are on a slippery slope here, in trying to interpret the nature of Christ. Man has never satisfactorily been able to describe the dynamics of the double nature of Christ as God and man. Some recent theology has tended to settle for an adoptionist Christology which sees Christ's divinity as a sort of cumulative result of his obedience to the Father. That attempt fails to do full justice to the divinity of Christ, but it is certainly useful in appreciating the fullness of his humanity. Such an anthropological bias is understandable in a culture for which supernatural categories have lost much of their power, but Christian theology cannot be content with a statement that does less than full justice to the divinity of Christ.

In a recent book, John MacQuarrie grapples with such difficulties with characteristic clarity.

> One of the most human of all activities is decision. Everyone, in the limited time at his disposal, has to make choices, to take up one vocation rather than another, to marry or to remain single and so on. To decide is a cutting away of some possibilities for the sake of the one that is chosen. Decision is to be understood as much [by] what is cut away as [by] what is chosen. In a finite existence, self-fulfilment is inseparable from self-denial.
>
> Perhaps when we talk of the 'fullness' of Christ, we have to look for it in this very matter of decision, so that the fullness is, paradoxically, also a self-emptying, a renunciation of other possibilities for the sake of that which has the greatest claim. Can we say that Christ's fullness or perfection was attributed to him because he gave up all other possibilities for the sake of the most distinctively human possibility of all, and the one that has most claim upon all men, namely, self-giving love? And can we also say that because this love is the most creative thing in human life, then Christ manifests the 'glory of man' by becoming transparent to the ultimate creative self-giving source of all, to God? And if indeed Christ is understood as the revelation of God, then this surely strengthens the argument

for a basic affinity between Christian and non-Christian morals (and here we could add non-Christian religious striving), for what is revealed or made clear in Christ is also implicit in the whole creation.[2]

However we interpret Christ's life, it was marked by an obedience to the Father that led to the cross. Christ rejected every temptation to dilute his perfect obedience to the Father. Again we are on the slippery slope, because Christ endured the cross for the sake of a kingdom that was not of this world. He was sorely tempted to give men the earthly substitutes they wanted. Indeed, there is enough in his teaching to intoxicate any utopian. Both the negative and positive evidence of his life and teaching, however, proves that the kingdom he offered men was only in a very elusive way a kingdom of this world. The fact and the manner of his death was the clearest proof of his conviction that the ultimate realities were spiritual and that they alone could lastingly satisfy man. It would profit a man nothing to gain the whole world and lose his soul. The only reality that endured was fellowship with God, and Jesus was the way to that fellowship. It was as if God had sent him forth to advertise in the most dramatic way that one thing only was needed, the love of God. It is true that he hinted that all other things would be added if love were pursued, but that is a puzzling addendum and not at all clear. As it was for Christ, those who love God most, often seem to draw to themselves the most suffering and persecution.

The only good that Christ came offering was the ultimate and only intrinsic good, God himself.

We can see Christ's life as a great placard set across the ages affirming to man that those hints and rumours from the Unseen whisper truly that, after all, only one thing is needful; that beneath the fascinating multiplicity of life there is *one* who calls them, and that only in him will they find their peace.

The matter is not left there for Christians. Christians do not merely look back to the memory of a man who endured to the end with total fidelity to God. History has many exemplary heroes, many who do the job better than Christ. Christ left behind very little formal teaching and much of that was unoriginal, a distillation of the wisdom of his race. We know little about his life, and most of what we do know is about his last week on earth. He gave little practical guidance on living and what he did say was highly paradoxical and liable to contradictory interpretations. When his disciples emerged from gloom and despair after his death they spent very little time in talking about his life at all! Instead, they are found proclaiming, not the manner of his life, but the fact of his resurrection! For the first Christians the real significance of Christ emerged after his death in his rising from the dead. The first Christians were first and foremost witnesses to the resurrection: 'You killed the prince of life. God, however, raised him from the dead, and to that fact we are the witnesses' (Acts 3.15).

The Christian Church found its *raison d'être* in the proclamation and celebration of the resurrection of Jesus Christ from the dead. God in Christ had admitted them to a share in the mystery of his purpose for all creation. God had revealed to them his hidden plan for the reconstitution of all things. The resurrection, however, was more than a glimpse into the future; it was more than a pledge; it was a beginning. Christ was the first-fruits; the first sheaf had already been harvested; the sickle had already been laid to the field. By a mystical engrafting into the living reality of the risen Christ they, too, partook of his resurrection.

> Since you have been brought back to true life with Christ, you must look for the things that are in heaven, where Christ is, sitting at God's right hand. Let your thoughts be on heavenly things, not on the things that are on the earth, because you have died, and now the life you have is hidden with Christ in God. But when Christ is revealed—and he is your life—you too will be revealed in all your glory with him. (Colossians 3.1-4)

The Church exists as a sign to point men to the secret of their own destiny. Yves Congar says, 'She is a gathering of men among other gatherings of men, but bearing among them the mystery of Jesus Christ. She is the company of witnesses to him . . . . She brings Christ to the world, offering it opportunities to recognise him as the key to its destiny!'[3] Eugene Hillman calls the Church 'the community of explicit faith in Christ'.

The Divine Saviour Himself enters into the condition of human bondage in order to re-make all of His creation from within, and to manifest His love to the eyes of flesh and give men hope through faith in the Christ Who is God with us. . . . In concrete historical terms, He accomplished, in the sight of some men, the salvation of all men. . . . This good news, however, has not yet reached all men unambiguously, through historically concrete and relevant symbols.

What remains now to be done in these 'latter days' is to make up what is still lacking in comparison with the sufferings already endured. . . . In union with the historic and trans-historic Christ, this community of explicit faith gives testimony to the universal reality of the messianic Kingdom within all those who have already responded or shall ever respond, to God's offer of saving grace made available in and through Christ to all mankind. . . . It is the community of Christian witnesses, the visible first fruits of salvation, designated beforehand by God for this very purpose, standing sacramentally for and among the whole people of God.[4]

The Church is an eschatalogical community, standing in history as a sign to all men of the destiny of creation. Her primary function is to bear witness by her life to the glory of God as shown in Christ. It follows that the definitive task of the Church is worship. She is a eucharistic community, engaged in celebrating God's mighty acts in creation and redemption. In our pragmatic and achievement-oriented culture that description of the Church is a stumbling-block. The aspects the Church's life most vaunted today are the derivative and not the essential ones. The Church is proclaimed to be a Servant Church, attending the needs of the world. That indeed is a true function of the Church, but it is not the first truth. In practice, where the Church has emphasised serving to the neglect of other parts of her life, she has ceased to minister to the real needs of man. Man cannot live without bread, but he dare not live by bread alone. If the Church abandons her ministry to spiritual needs, men soon turn to substitutes. It is no accident that the decline of spirituality in Western Christianity has coincided with the emergence of a whole series of bogus spiritualities. At best, the spiritually hungry have ransacked Eastern mysticism and at worst they have fallen into the destructive frenzy of the psychedelic drug scene. Man was not made to live within himself. He has to learn to go out from himself, to be ecstatic; and only through a genuine spirituality can he do so sanely. In the final chapter I shall outline the old tested way to a renewed spirituality. Meanwhile, we must discuss the Church as a worshipping fellowship.

14

Worship

THERE ARE levels of human experience, just as there are certain ideas and theories, that cannot be defined except by means of themselves. Definition normally proceeds by reduction to more basic elements. For instance, the colour purple is reducible to the colours red and blue, but red and blue are not reducible beyond their own basic redness and blueness. They are primary colours, irreducible, red is red, and blue is blue. In language, there are many words which are reducible to other words; but there are certain basic elements in language that we cannot get beyond. Those primary elements make language and discourse possible. Without them discourse would be impossible because men would be engaged in an endless regress. There are certain areas of experience which we simply have to take for granted. They are the foundation upon which everything else is built. They reflect a basic reality, and they save us from the prison of ourselves and endless relativity.

In the same way, there are certain human experiences that are good in themselves and are not to be thought of as serving any end beyond themselves. In the language of ethics, the distinction is between instrumental good and intrinsic good. An instrumental good is something good *for* something else; it acts as a lever upon a further good. Aspirin is not good in itself. It is good for headaches if and when you have them. An intrinsic good is an end in itself. It is sought for its own sake and not because it leads toward a higher good.

In our radically utilitarian culture, many see that distinction only as a stalking-horse for metaphysics and the supernatural. Our culture loves to relativise everything, because absolutes and first principles have all sorts of unpredictable power. They pull down man's vanity by putting him under the judgement of external values. When man makes himself and his projects the measure of all things, he must try to undermine the structure of objective values and first principles.

An instructive example is the attack on artists and intellectuals in the Soviet Union. According to the Marxist theory the only thing that is good in itself is the State, so art must be made to serve the ends of the government. Obviously that idea hits at the very essence of art. It denies the integrity of the artist, who must resist anything that would compromise his vision. John Drury has said that artists, thinkers, scientists and lovers 'are *contra mundum*. They separate themselves from ordinary distraction, sometimes to the point of eccentricity. Called absent-minded, they are in fact present-minded, because they do this in order to be present with some particular point of the world—to love it and know it . . . . The resistance is in the service of knowing and recognising.'[1] An artist who allows his art to become an instrumental good has ceased to be a pure artist.

A similar debate is going on in Britain and the USA over the good of education. How far is education an instrumental good and how far is it an intrinsic good? Should the university be radicalised and made to serve the cause of revolution? How far may the academic rightly withdraw from ordinary distractions for the sake of his scholarship? Those are momentous questions and they force themselves on the Church as well. Is the Church an instrumental good or an instrinsic good, or both? How far and to what extent may she operate as a pressure group for social or political ends? There are no easy or simple answers.

All of which is immediately relevant to the Church's primary task of worship. A 'theology of surrender' makes worship problematic. Where the supernatural has been explicitly or implicitly rejected the whole reason for worship is removed. As noted in chapter 2, the supernatural 'denotes a fundamental category of religion, namely the assertion of belief that there is another reality, and one of ultimate significance for man, which transcends the reality within which our everyday experience unfolds.'[2]

Worship is the basic and instinctive response of man

to the transcendent reality of God. It is not an instrumental category at all, and that is what poses the greatest problem for certain schools in modern theology. Worship, like art, resists external control and manipulation. It is thus a challenge and an irritation to totalitarians anywhere, in the realms of politics or ideas. Any regime that moves against the Church begins by banning worship, and logically so, because worship implies a resistance against every power save the power of God. The man who worships God is a threat to every other power which claims absolute authority. Where the sense of the majesty and reality of God is lacking, worship becomes problematic, because, like art, it fares badly in any attempt to instrumentalise it. In the absence of a vivid awareness of the supernatural, the temptation is to retain worship as an instrumental good—as a stimulant to good behaviour, or a device for producing fellowship, or a celebration of human interpersonal relationships—somehow to locate its significance in the worshipper. That is precisely what worship is not.

The purpose of worship is not simply to produce a kind of instant fellowship. Worship is not simply a decorous social event, a sort of stylised family party or liturgical barbecue. Nor is the purpose of worship to evoke beautiful thoughts or stimulate its practitioners to more strenuous moral effort. Nor is worship a device for evoking patriotism or for promoting national self-identity. Worship is not auto-suggestion.

Worship may and in fact does have elements of all those things, but none of them is its purpose. Such a concept of worship would locate the meaning of worship in us—in our self-concern, in our relationships, in our self-improvement, even in our good works. The beginning and end of worship, however, is in the great and glorious being of God. In worship we respond to the initiative of God by acts of adoring self-offering. It is important to understand every word in that statement. The primary movement in worship is God's. Worship begins beyond time in a movement of the Eternal Charity, an utterance of the Word.

> For while all things were in quiet silence and the night was in the midst of her swift course, Thine Almighty word leaped down from heaven out of thy royal throne. (Wisdom 18.14-15)

One thinker even described God as not only the object of worship, but also the subject. The movement of which our worship is a part begins in God. God's initiative becomes revelation, the disclosing of God. On man's side worship is his response to that revelation, that approach. His response is the adoring self-offering of the creature to the eternal.

I want to underline two fundamentals here. The first is that worship, authentic worship, is the acknowledgement of a reality independent of the worshipper, a reality which is always coloured by mystery, which is there first, and which approaches man. As Evelyn Underhill wrote in *Worship:* 'In other words, it is the

implicit, even though unrecognised Vision of God—
that disclosure of the Supernatural which is overwhelming, self-giving and attractive all at once—
which is the first cause of all worship, from the puzzled
upward glance of the primitive to the delighted self-
oblation of the saint.'[3]

Worship presupposes and is the response to the self-
disclosure, however veiled, of the reality of God. That
is fundamental. Any approach that disallows that
reality or reduces its primacy, may be some sort of
valuable ethico-cultural experience, but it is not worship. The second point to notice is, on the human side,
the disinterested quality of worship. It is true that
human activity is ambiguous, a mixture of self-regard
and disinterestedness, but self-regard has no real, no
essential part in worship. Man's needs and wishes are
not what evoke worship. The essence of worship is
not asking or even talking, but offering and adoration.
The seraphic hymn gives its very essence: 'Holy, holy,
holy, Lord God of Hosts, heaven and earth are full of
thy glory; glory be to thee O Lord most high.' It
always strikes me that, whatever their origin, two
words presently used in English worship that best express the note of exultant, unself-regarding adoration,
are utterly useless for any other purpose: the words
hosanna and *hallelujah*!

Because worship is the adoring self-offering of each
man to his Creator, in which he joins the praise of the
whole creation, we can expect it to be as wide and as

rich as human nature itself. I love those first lines of one of Hopkins' sonnets celebrating the glorious diversity of creation: 'Glory be to God for dappled things.' Beneath the variety of scene is the same pulse of adoration. Not only will the self-offering be as wide as the varieties of men, it will be as inclusive as each man is himself. Each of us is a creature of many parts, body as well as mind and heart, and the body has many senses. Each bears its portion of praise. Our worship should be an offering of the mind, but not just an exercise in cerebration. Men and women are more than souls with ears, as W. G. Davies once remarked, though the flight from the body in Protestant culture seems to suggest that the ears are the only members of the body safe to indulge! Worship is an offering of the eyes and ears and nose and even more. The beauty of movement, the glory of music, the offering of incense—all can be part of our self-offering as we bring to God the totality of our being, leaving nothing out, ashamed of nothing.

Here there is recognition that man is an embodied creature of flesh and blood, that Christianity is a religion of incarnation, that we learn through our senses as well as through our minds. The whole aim of the sacramental life is not so much instruction as incorporation, and this in turn fights against all individualism and subjectivism and teaches appreciation for the objective substance of the faith.[4]

We are creatures who need order and control in our lives, so we can expect our worship to be disciplined and traditional, using the family prayers of the household of God down the ages. Because we are free spirits, our worship must also be free and spontaneous in order to avoid the pitfalls of being too formalised and liturgical. Finding the balance between the two aspects of worship is a perennial problem. No Church has found the perfect balance, and different traditions preserve necessary emphases.

Surely in our worship we can find a place for the offering of silence. Father Kelly of Kelham used to say, 'He who cannot keep silence is not content with God.' We must try to restore silence and stillness to our worship (and an inner silence and stillness is possible even in the presence of small children).

However long we spend at it, worship like art cannot, really be defined or described—it can only be experienced. The real heart of Christian worship is, of course, the eucharistic liturgy. The liturgy, like the Church herself, can be understood only eschatologically. In the liturgy the Church acts as the world's priest, solemnly remembering and representing before God his mighty acts in creation and redemption. The word *remember* is itself an eschatological term here. To appreciate its depth, we must leave our human way of experiencing time as past, present, and future. We tend to think of time as the unfolding of a newsreel. When we remember something, we look back to an event which is made present to the memory by a process of imagined recall. When we remember events, we are clearly no longer able to participate in them. Such temporal categories do not help us at all in understanding the Church's 'remembering' before God. In fact, we all experience time in different ways. When I was in the army, we used to tick off the days one by one till we would be home again. Time was like a great weight we longed to be freed from. Then there are times that we're not conscious of time at all, when time seems to stand still. When you're with someone you love and are deeply happy with, all is a gloriously vivid Now. It is a glimpse into eternity, a foretaste of heaven, because in God there is no time, no beginning and no ending, only the timeless joy of an eternal present. When God revealed himself to Moses he gave his name as 'I am that I am. Tell them I am sent you.' God proclaimed himself timelessly present, eternally self-existent. It is impossible for our time-bound minds to grasp even the edges of that truth, but we must try to understand that in God there is no past and no future—only a joyously vivid present. God's mighty acts in creation and redemption are not just events in the past, as they seem from our temporal standpoint. They are gathered together in the eternal present of God's love. In the liturgy the Church is not looking back to the past. She is engaging herself to an endlessly present reality in which she enters the mystery of God's purpose. That is why any adequate eucharistic liturgy is not experienced as a memorial meal which looks back to the past, but as a foretaste and pledge of the glorious future which God is even now bringing to pass. That way of experiencing the liturgy avoids the debate about the nature of the Real Presence in the elements. Certain definitions and counter-definitions of the Real Presence make the fatal mistake of trying to contain the eternal within temporal categories. The action of the liturgy is Godward. We do not conjure up God's presence. He raises *us* to *his* presence in heaven. The liturgy is a much deeper mystery than the polemicists have allowed. The action of the liturgy is not 'by conversion of Godhead into flesh: but by taking Manhood into God.'

It is obvious that the sense of the awe-fulness of worship can exist only among a fellowship of those for whom God is a vivid and present reality. All the great liturgies evolved in the context of such awe. Today's liturgies tend to be thin and subjective by comparison. Modern liturgies, like much modern architecture, seem to have all the right elements in the right places, but they do not lift the heart. They are schoolboy themes, not poetry; diagrams, not art. They are intellectual constructions, and the mind alone can never contain the mysterium of God.

While we may be thankful for much in the liturgical renewal, especially for everything that gives to the Eucharist a more central place in the Church's life, many innovations have been instituted without considering their symbolic meaning—indeed, often the intended and symbolic meanings are in conflict. One such practice is the adoption of the westward position by the celebrant. That position, we are told, is to be preferred because it focuses attention upon a point in the middle. It seems actually a strong reflection of modern subjectivism. If a real God, transcending man and to whom one may offer worship, has become doubtful, then we must turn in upon ourselves and meditate on our own humanity and what is going on in our midst. That, however, is not what the reformers think they are doing. They urge rather that the Church should turn outward and look beyond itself![5]

We must be patient. God's glory has a disconcerting habit of breaking through those who are least aware of themselves. Today's Church is too self-conscious to be a very effective vessel for revelation, too boringly and unremittingly aware of itself and the impression it is making. But who knows? God uses the most unlikely instruments to bring us to our knees. The bankruptcies of the 60s may yet teach us that the Church has never had and never will have any sufficiency of itself. It is good only for one thing—to rejoice in its own weakness and to witness to God's greater glory.

Divine folly is wiser than the wisdom of man, and divine weakness stronger than man's strength. My brothers, think what sort of people you are, whom God has called. Few of you are men of wisdom, by any human standard; few are powerful or highly born. Yet, to shame the wise, God has chosen what the world counts folly, and to shame what is strong, God has chosen what the world counts weakness. He has chosen things low and contemptible,

154

mere nothings, to overthrow the existing order. And so there is no place for human pride in the presence of God. You are in Christ Jesus *by God's Act*, for God has made *him* our wisdom; *he* is our righteousness; *in him* we are consecrated and set free. And so (in the words of scripture), 'If a man is proud, let him be proud of the Lord.' (I Corinthians I.25–31)

15

Prayer

MAN IS a complicated creature. He is obviously part of nature: he is born, he procreates, and he dies. All that he shares with the animal creation from which he is descended. Like the animals he has instincts and drives. A large part of every day is spent on servicing our poor old body and its needs—Brother Ass, as St Francis compassionately called it. We belong to the great unconscious world of nature. Like everything in nature we change and decay. 'We spring up like the grass which today is, and tomorrow is cast into the oven.' There is, however, one massive difference between ourselves and the rest of nature. My very ability to describe the animal side of my nature is proof enough that I am more than an animal. I am a *conscious* animal.

It is hard to define exactly what *conscious* really means, but look at it like this: as far as we can tell, an animal is not aware of itself as an individual at all. It is part of the impersonal flow of nature. It is unlikely, for instance, that animals know they are going to die. The animal has no hopes. It cannot stand outside itself and think about its own life and plan for it and seek to understand it; but man has the strange gift of consciousness. We are part of nature, but something in us enables us to transcend nature, to stand outside of nature, outside of ourselves, and appraise both. Man, then, is trapped in nature, in the unconscious drive of life, and yet, he is above nature, transcending it, superior to it. He is a bit like God in that he can look on the world from outside. That is what differentiates us from the rest of creation and characterises us as human beings. Several things follow.

First of all, what we call 'morality' follows. The truly human person is the person in whom consciousness controls nature. To take an extreme example: the promiscuous person, who leads a life of disordered sexual indulgence, is not yet truly and completely human, because his human consciousness is not what controls and dominates his life, but his instinctive nature. The truly human person is the one able to transcend and direct his natural impulses according to his own choosing. His instincts and natural impulses don't rule and dominate him; he rules and dominates them. As Plato said, human nature is like a man driving a chariot pulled by very powerful horses. The horses are the natural appetites. The driver in the chariot is the mind or consciousness of man and he holds the reins. Now, two things can happen. The horses can bolt and pull man and the chariot anywhere they like in a headlong and pointless gallop. That happens.

Some men are pulled this way and that by their appetites and drives. There is no control, no direction, no purpose in their lives. On the other hand, there is the man who drives like a good charioteer. He controls the horses, he drives them, points them in the direction he wants them to take, and makes them work for him. He is the truly human man, the man in whom consciousness and reason are in control. The truly human man is the moral man.

Secondly, there follows something of even greater importance. Only man of all the creatures is able to understand and direct his nature; and only man of all the creatures is able to understand the mystery of his own origin. He alone is able to meditate on why and by whom he was created. The psalms and canticles are full of talk about nature praising or magnifying God: 'The heavens declare the glory of God,' or 'O all ye works of the Lord bless ye the Lord. O ye seas and floods bless ye the Lord. O ye beasts and cattle bless ye the Lord, O all ye green things upon earth bless ye the Lord, praise him and magnify him for ever.' Such praise and worship of God by nature is, however, unconscious. The beasts and cattle, the green things upon earth, glorify God unconsciously. Man is different, able to be moral or immoral because he has consciousness. That brings us to our second truly human activity —prayer.

The truly human man is moral, and the truly human man is a man of prayer. Those two activities define man as a human being, and set him apart from the rest of creation. Man is truly human when he is moral and when he prays, because at those two points he is asserting his human consciousness over his blind, instinctive, and impulsive nature. When a man prays he draws himself back from the flood and pressure of instinct and nature and acts as pure consciousness, as pure spirit. The real man of prayer as he prays becomes unaware of the weight and pull of his natural self. He tastes, for a moment, the purest humanity. Deep calls to deep, his spirit communes with the spirit of God, the world falls away, and his soul rests alone with God. That is to be truly human.

> The man who prays has to go into his room and shut the door, both to be with his Father who is in secret and to exclude the insistent voices of fashionable witch-doctors, his own distractions, and not least the admonitions of anxious orthodoxy. The courage to do this can only come from the assurance that he matters as he is, and this assurance is itself a gift of God in prayer, something he must always ask for and receive.[1]

If you accept that morality and prayer are the two most characteristically human activities, then you'll expect them to be the most difficult—and they are. Our instinctive, natural man is always pulling against the creation of a real and true humanity in our natures. How often does our instinctive nature cry out against the demands of that human control which is morality! We are often like the charioteer fighting to control those powerful horses. Our arms weary of reining them in, of fighting them in the direction we want them to take. It seems much easier to let them have their head, to eat and sleep when they demand, to drink or drug ourselves at their insistence, to give our sexual appetites a free run if they want it, to allow our tongue, our malice, our spitefulness to rage on unchecked. Morality is a hard and often bitter struggle, and so is prayer. Prayer demands incredible efforts. It means to pull yourself apart, drag yourself away from all the responsibilities and fascinations of purely natural living and engage in the painful exercise of stillness and quietness, of attentive listening, of waiting on God. We'll do anything to avoid it. Yet in prayer the highest expression of humanity is reached. The man who is, in the old Scottish saying, 'far ben wi' God', is recognised as man as he is really meant to be, man at his highest, man at his most manly.

Most of us recognise that. Most of us want to be men of prayer. Yet how do we start? The whole thing seems incredibly difficult, but there are things we can start doing straight away. Prayer is a practice, not a theory, and the Christian tradition has a wealth of advice available for us to use.

The first lesson we must learn is that prayer, real prayer, prayer that lives and grows, requires discipline and regularity. There's no prayer without tears, prayer without effort. One of the saddest things about the drug sub-culture is its attempts to attain spiritual vision without effort and discipline and waiting. There are dozens of instant spiritualities around today. They witness to man's need to pray, but they want prayer to be easy. Prayer, in fact, is the hardest activity there is and it requires regular discipline. Prayer is like learning a new language or learning to play a musical instrument. You can't just do it when you feel like it. Musicians and linguists have behind them years of sheer drudging effort. Even when they reach a high standard, they are not finished. The price of excellence is constant practice, endless discipline. To pray, then, the first thing to do is sit down and plan your daily schedule with places for prayer. There is no point at all in leaving it to chance or feeling, because the chances rarely come. You need to make time for prayer, and if you want to make progress, you'll have to make quite a bit of time.

For simplicity's sake, we can divide prayer into two levels. The first I'll call 'the Prayer of Greeting'. It is the equivalent of human courtesies that mark our daily life: 'Good morning, John, how are you today? I see Celtic beat Leeds last night. Well, see you later. Goodbye.' Banal. Small-talk. The courtesies are observed, the channels of communication are kept open, with the promise of a good visit at the weekend. As in everyday living we greet people, engage in small-talk, and then get on with our work, we should do the same with God. He knows how busy we are, better than our friends do; but like them, he doesn't like to be cut dead or ignored just because we're rushing off somewhere. There's always time for a brief acknowledgement of friendship and dependence—the equivalent of the husbandly kiss during the headlong rush to the front door. We should set aside a brief space every day to greet God in that way. Two minutes in the morning and two in the evening will do. That kind of banal prayer keeps the channels open and the relationship alive till we get time for more. What do we say? Well, there are plenty of suggestions around. Most manuals of prayer have morning and evening sections, and the Prayer Book itself contains many ancient and beautiful prayers. Here are two examples.

Morning: O Lord our heavenly Father, Almighty and Everlasting God, who hast safely brought us to the beginning of this day: Defend us in the same with thy mighty power; and grant that this day we fall into no sin, neither run into any kind of danger; but that all our doings may be ordered by thy governance, to do always that is righteous in thy sight.

Evening: Be present, O merciful God, and protect us through the silent hours of this night, so that we who are wearied by the changes and chances of this fleeting world may repose upon thy eternal changelessness.

That is one level of prayer and in many ways it is the most important, but it is obviously not enough. No friendship can grow and develop unless there is time for real conversation. Obviously we must take time to get to know God. We need what I'll call 'the prayer of Communion'. As conversation takes longer than small-talk so does this type of prayer. So we must consult our schedules again. So far we've pencilled in a mere two minutes, morning and evening. Now we must reserve a full hour, either a solid hour or two half-hour periods, no less. You can't develop a relationship of love with anyone on less than one hour a week, and certainly not with God. One hour. We probably spend more watching television, or doing crosswords, or reading novels, or playing games, or drinking beer or coffee. Can we honestly grudge one hour a week from such pursuits to get to know God? Once we've found the hour, however, we must stick to it.

The two levels of prayer, then, are the brief prayer of greeting, and the longer prayer of Communion. Now, *where* do we pray? Obviously, the prayer of greeting will be done at home. We greet people where we are, whenever we bump into them. The prayer of greeting may be done wherever we are first thing in the morning and last thing at night. That's usually in our bedrooms, though it can be anywhere.

The prayer of Communion is different, however. We usually have conversation with people when we visit them or when they visit us. It is not just a casual meeting; it is a planned meeting. We think out in advance where we are going to meet, where we won't be interrupted and that's where we talk. It is the same with the prayer of Communion. We plan the place and home may not be, probably isn't, the best place.

It may be too noisy, or too distracting, or too small. So we make special arrangements.

Churches are left open for just this kind of prayer. Church buildings are out of fashion today because, humanly speaking, they are pretty useless. They are meant only to be prayed in, and where prayer has lost its meaning they become embarrassing. They stand as parables of our loss. I find churches the best place to pray in and I am glad to find support, of a sort, from Philip Larkin's poem, 'Church Going':

> A serious house on serious earth it is,
> In whose blent air all our compulsion meet,
> Are recognized, and robed as destinies,
> And that much never can be obsolete,
> Since someone will forever be surprising
> A hunger in himself to be more serious,
> And gravitating with it to this ground,
> Which, he once heard, was proper to grow wise in,
> If only that so many dead lie round.[2]

As an added refinement, choose a dark church, if you can, since according to John Donne in 'A Hymne To Christ,'

> Churches are best for Prayer, that have least light:
> To see God only, I goe out of sight:
> And to scape stormy dayes, I chuse
> An Everlasting night.

In any event, these are the essentials: a regular time and suitable place. The regular discipline of brief daily prayer and longer weekly prayer. Now, to make sure that we don't spend the longer periods in wool-gathering and day-dreaming, more has to be said about how to use the time.

I have already suggested a parallel between learning prayer and learning a new language. The best way to learn a language is by imitation. That is how we learned to speak. We imitated the sounds our parents made. We did what they did. That is how we start learning the language of prayer. I want to suggest three ways of praying, though there are many more, and we can learn most of them by imitating others, by copying what they do.

First, there is prayer of the lips, or vocal prayer. Next there is prayer of the mind, or mental prayer. Then there is the prayer of silence, probably the truest kind of prayer there is.

1. Vocal prayer is fairly simple to describe and easy to imitate. It consists of saying prayers out loud or under your breath. It is the best way to begin, but to do it you'll need a book. If you are going to take the life of prayer seriously, you must build up a small collection of books on prayer. There are many excellent ones. One of the best is the lovely book by the late Dean of York, Eric Milner White, *My God my Glory*. It is filled with many beautiful prayers, written or collected by a real man of God. There are many other books. Find one you like and learn to use it regularly. The method is simple. You read over the chosen

prayer slowly and thoughtfully. Let your mind linger on the words and the meaning behind them. If some words catch your interest, stay with them, pondering them until you want to move on. You can use the psalms in the same way. That's really all that's to it. Using the prayers others have used, imitating their example. The prayer of the lips.

2. The prayer of the mind is more complicated and some people never master it at all. It is thinking about God or Jesus or one of the saints and trying to apply what we learn to our own lives. Meditation should always end in a practical resolve to do something. Here is an example of a simple method of meditation.

Take a passage from the Bible or an event in our Lord's life and look at it in three ways, under three headings: God before my eyes. God in my heart. God in my hands. For instance, think of the death of Christ. Apply the three headings. *God before my eyes.* What do I learn about God from the death of Jesus Christ? What do I see of God before my eyes in that event? I see a God who loves me so much that he gives me his beloved son for my salvation. I see a love that loves till death. That is the kind of God I see before my eyes. A loving God. A God who loves and loves and loves till death.

God in my heart. What does it all say to me, to my own heart, about my life? It is my sin that crucifies him. My selfishness, my greed, my spite, my lack of forgiveness. I must crucify those parts of me. I must deny them, cross them out. There is maybe one sin, one weakness in particular which I have to deny in myself. Some part of me has to be crucified today. I must resolve to deny some part of myself today.

God in my hands. What does the passage teach me about my duty to my neighbour? My duty to God's world. Do I love my neighbour? Do I forgive him? Do I give myself to the needs of God's children? Is God in my hands to the world, or is he locked up in my heart? What particular deed must I do today to bring God in my hands to the world?

That's the prayer of the mind, meditation. It takes quite a bit of practice, but we can learn from others. There are books of meditation. There are notes for Bible study. There's the Bible. People complain about not understanding the Bible. Well, Mark Twain once remarked that it wasn't the bits of the Bible he didn't understand that worried him; it was the bits he did. There are plenty of those—enough to spend a life-time meditating upon.

3. Finally, there's the prayer of silence, sometimes called the prayer of simplicity because it is so simple. Bishop Bloom repeats the following story. Once the Curé D'Ars, a French saint of the nineteenth century, asked an old peasant what he was doing sitting for hours in the church, seemingly not even praying. The peasant replied, 'I look at him, he looks at me, and we are happy together.' That was the prayer of silence. The prayer of simplicity, however, is not easy. What

you do is to empty your mind of everything that is not God. All the things that worry or excite or anger you—put them all away and fix your mind quietly on God. Don't even talk to him. Just fix your attention on him, be at home with him. It is very hard to do. Our minds are full of things and, as soon as we try to pray, they bob up. When that happens, don't entertain them; don't let them get started. Quietly remove them. Tell them they can come in later, but not now. If you persevere a little at a time, it'll come. If you can build into your week little enclosures of silence, they'll gradually spill over into your life and bring that peace which the world cannot give—the peace of God.

Prayer is still possible, even for a generation for whom God often seems to be in eclipse, since God is still near to each one of us. Each generation is still equidistant from God. Our generation merely has less patience, and there is no prayer without patience.

NOTES

CHAPTER 1

1 Peter L. Berger, *A Rumour of Angels* (New York: Doubleday, 1969), p. 7
2 St Augustine, *Confessions*, Volume 11

CHAPTER 2

1 Berger, op. cit., p. 12
2 Ibid., p. 2
3 Quoted in Paul van Buren, *Secular Meaning of the Gospel* (London: S.C.M.), p. 94
4 Ibid., p. 96
5 Richard Rubinstein, *The Secular City Debate* (New York: MacMillan, 1966), p. 132
6 *New York Times*
7 Ibid
8 *New Christian*

CHAPTER 3

1 Ian Fraser, *Let's Get Moving* (Scottish Churches Council, 1969)
2 Ibid., pp. 36–39
3 Quoted in Herbert Butterfield, *Christianity and History* (London: G. Bell and Sons Ltd., 1950), p. 66

CHAPTER 4

1 E. Schillebeeckx, *Christ the Sacrament of Encounter with God* (New York: Sheed & Ward, 1963), pp. 6, 8
2 Eugene Hillman, *The Church as Mission* (New York: Herder & Herder, 1965), p. 98
3 John MacQuarrie, 'Subjectivity and Objectivity in Theology and Worship.' *Theology*, November 1969, Vol. LXXII, Nol 593, pp. 501, 502
4 Evelyn Underhill, *An Anthology of the Love of God* (London: A. R. Mowbray & Co. Ltd., 1953), p. 123 ff.
5 Karl Rahner, S.J., quoted in Hillman, op. cit., p. 84
6 Hillman, op. cit., pp. 50, 51

CHAPTER 5

1 Richard Niebuhr, *Christ and Culture* (New York: Harper Torchbooks, 1956), p. 40
2 Freya Stark, *Rome on the Euphrates*, p. 56
3 Daniel Boorstin, *The Image* (Penguin Books, 1961), p. 53

CHAPTER 6

1 Erich Fromm, *Ye Shall Be As Gods* (New York: Rinehart and Winston, 1966), p. 70
2 John Hick, *Evil and the God of Love* (New York: Harper and Row, 1966), p. 317
3 Ibid., p. 319
4 Ibid
5 Eric Mascall, *Theology and the Future* (London: Darton, Longman & Todd, 1968), p. 56
6 Schubert M. Ogden, *The Reality of God* (New York: Harper and Row, 1966), p. 31
7 Ibid., pp. 41-2
8 Augustine, op cit

CHAPTER 7

1 Arthur Miller, *Collected Plays* (New York: Viking Press, 1961), p. 222
2 C. S. Lewis, *The Weight of Glory* (London: S.P.C.K., 1954), p. 8
3 Lewis, op. cit., p. 10
4 Augustine, op. cit.

CHAPTER 8

1 Andre Malraux, *Man's Estate* (London and Harmondsworth: Methuen and Penguin, 1948) quoted by Ladislaus Boros, *The Mystery of Death* (New York: Herder and Herder, 1965), p. vii
2 Dylan Thomas, *Miscellany One* (London: J. M. Dent and Sons Ltd., 1965), p. 31
3 Ignace Lepp, *Death and its Mysteries* (London: Burns and Oates, 1969), pp. 7, 8
4 John MacQuarrie, *Studies in Christian Existentialism* (Philadelphia: The Westminster Press, 1965), p. 51
5 Ibid., p. 54
6 Edgar Allan Poe
7 Miguel De Unamuno, *The Tragic Sense of Life* (New York: Dover Publications, 1954), p. 43
8 Boros, op. cit., p. 84
9 Ibid., p. 53

10 Ibid., pp. 58, 59
11 MacQuarrie, op. cit., p. 7 (cited from *L'Etre at le Néant*, Paris: Gallimard, 1945, pp. 708, 721)
12 Bertrand Russell, *Autobiography* (Boston: Little, Brown and Company, 1967), p. 3

CHAPTER 9

1 Eric Mascall, op. cit., pp. 57, 58
2 William Temple, *Revelation*, p. 107
3 Ibid

CHAPTER 11

1 See William Barclay, *Crucified and Crowned* (London: SCM Press, 1967), pp. 31 ff.

CHAPTER 12

1 John MacQuarrie, *An Existentialist Theology* (New York: Harper and Row, 1965), p. 185 f.
2 Frederick Buechner, *The Magnificent Defeat* (New York: The Seabury Press), p. 79 f.
3 Quoted in Mascall, op. cit., p. 183

CHAPTER 13

1 E. Schillebeeckx, *The Layman in the Church* (New York: Alba House, 1963), p. 64
2 John MacQuarrie, *Three Issues in Ethics* (London: SCM, 1970), pp. 87, 88
3 Hillman, op. cit., p. 129
4 Ibid., pp. 130, 131

CHAPTER 14

1 John Drury in *The Phenomenon of Christian Belief*, Ed. G. W. Lampe (London: Mowbrays, 1970), p. 95
2 Berger, op. cit., p. 2
3 Evelyn Underhill, *Worship*, Collins, 1962
4 John MacQuarrie, 'Subjectivity and Objectivity in Worship.' In *Theology*, Nov. 1969, p. 503
5 Ibid., p. 504—where the ideas and many of the words of this paragraph have their origin.

CHAPTER 15

1 Drury, op. cit., p. 96
2 Philip Larkin, 'Church Going,' in *The Penguin Book of Contemporary Verse*, p. 337